# A ROAD IN MY NAME

## REAL LIFE TIPS THAT WILL HELP YOU GROW FASTER.

RAKESH SINGH

ISBN
Hardcase 979-8-89673-700-1
Paperback 979-8-89610-954-9

# A Road in My Name

Real-life tips that will help you grow faster.

Everyone has a plan, but outcomes are not always as per the plan.

As an aspirant youth trying to make your career and a plan for a successful life. Things don't always turn out the way we expect them to. With so much competition around and scarcity of resources, what can we do differently so that everyone can get a chance to be successful, as an entrepreneur or a leader.

Rakesh Singh, a known business leader, author, investor, and philanthropist with broad experience in leading Fortune 500 companies, will share his lessons and tips that will guide you through navigating between the problem and roadblock but keep moving towards your goal in a shorter and faster way.

In *A Road In My Name*, Rakesh shares the insights from his real-life examples that will help you meet your goals and achieve them faster.

# Shout-out!

This book is dedicated to my mother, who is mostly responsible for building a strong character and discipline in me. She was the only person who consistently believed that I would be successful one day.

A big shout-out to my father, brother, and sisters for making me who I am today. Especially Dad for giving me a free hand.

I would like to thank my wife for inspiring me to write this book and my son and daughter for being my critics.

I want to thank and acknowledge my friends and peers who took time to make contributions. This wasn't possible without your help.

**"Maatr Vandna, Jai Mata Di"**

# Contents

# When Work Is Worship

*To be successful, the first thing to do is to fall in love with your work. – Sister Mary Lauretta*

I love going to work. Absolutely love it. That dialogue from Forrest Gump about life being a box of chocolates and you never know what to expect from it? That's work for me. Some days I'm learning the ropes, other days I'm leading companies into the tech age. And then some days, I meet people who've compelled me to write this book.

I am a technology leader for many Fortune 500 companies globally. Thanks to my work, I've become a chatty person who finds it easy to strike up conversations. That's how I ended up talking to a young man working for a service provider based in NOIDA, India. I had arrived in NOIDA for an operational assessment and came across him in the canteen. As we shared a table at lunch, he told me that he had joined the company a few months ago fresh out of college. As a BTech graduate, he was working at an entry-level job, which in IT firms means barely any application of the mind or skills. Early starters work in shifts, stare at the computer till the workday ends, and go home. He spoke of his excitement for his future: becoming a team leader, getting an MBA degree, and then the manager designation. He had his career all mapped out. Unfortunately, it was nothing different from everyone else his age who worked in IT. He didn't seem to know much about the tech world. He saw a path millions had taken before him and decided that that was for him too.

Our talk continued, and he told me that his father owned a furniture business. It was a conventional family business; his grandfather had started it, and his father took it ahead. But the young man wasn't interested in being a part of the legacy. Now I was hooked, and he faced a volley of questions. Where did they procure the raw materials from? Who were their customers? What about the inventory? Who were his father's ideal customers? As we continued speaking, it seemed like he was getting curious about the business he had grown up around all his life.

We were almost done with lunch, and I told him that his father's business sounded far more exciting than what he planned for himself. He'd be better off getting an MBA in supply chain management and joining the business. We spoke about that a bit more before I had to leave. A couple of years later, I learnt that he had, in fact, followed my advice and that the business was doing better than it ever had.

This young man's experience is more common than we think. India is full of people who don't quite know what they're doing and what they're looking for. And in the process, they're late to the story of their own lives. I was one of them.

This book is a guide for young people to expedite their journey towards success. It's a book I wish I'd had when I was out of college and struggling to find the one profession that would make my days more exciting. I thought I knew what I was always meant to do because since I was a child, I wanted to be a fighter pilot for the Indian Air Force. My father was employed there, and I saw that world from close quarters. I appeared for the qualifying exams with dedication and sincerity, but even though I qualified for the UPSC exam, I didn't clear the Staff Selection Board (SSB) interview thrice. The death of my childhood dream meant I had to pivot hard.

However, I knew nothing else except preparing to become a fighter pilot. That stubborn mindset—which I would now call near-sightedness—of putting all my eggs in one basket left me unqualified for anything else. I had no Plan B. I floundered from one profession to another—from graphic designer to call centre employee—before stumbling upon the one that was perfect for me: information technology. Along the way, I worked for the National Institute of Information Technology (NIIT), tech giants Wipro, Computer Associates (now Broadcom), Microsoft, Tata Consultancy Services, Cognizant Technologies and Countrywide which later became the Bank of America, among others. But to reach this happy state, I wasted precious years in my twenties. It's a time young people usually use to build a foundation for their careers. I spent that unsure of myself and my skills and what the future would hold.

I don't want others to make the mistakes I did. I have counselled many youngsters I've met through work, but I have limited reach in my small world. With the book, I can hopefully impact many, many more. My family has its roots in the state of Bihar, once known for its glorious history with Ashoka, Chanakya, and the Buddha, but which is now not doing too well on most national metrics. And since people make a place, it's them that we look towards when we talk about bringing any sort of positive change. Today's youth have great potential but not really the patience to see it through. Youngsters from UP and Bihar are known for their mathematics and scientific temperament, and the ones who do well are those who pursue the civil services. The two states' success rate is a testament to their potential. But what about those who can't crack the tough examinations? The masses there are pretty directionless, one of the reasons they end up in menial jobs which is a waste of their potential and far below what they are actually capable of.

This book is for them. I want them to see the big picture. To introspect. To break the pattern. To move away from the tried-and-tested route. And to know that making a living and achieving personal greatness is possible and can happen faster than they imagine.

When I first thought about writing a book that helps others through the trajectory of my career experiences, I went about it backwards. Usually, authors write their book and then come up with a title that sums it up. But not me. I initially planned to write this book in Hindi, calling it Ek Sadak Mere Naam. So A Road In My Name is the dream I have for my life. All around the world, governments and civil society celebrate noteworthy personalities by naming streets in their honour. They have given back to society, and society has celebrated their achievements. The driving force of my life is to do something that impacts lives in India and changes them for the better. So what can I do that gets me a road named after me too? I've already started working towards it. And this book is but a small part of it.

Now I am a technology leader, entrepreneur, investor, philanthropist, and author. It's incredible I've achieved so much, considering the bumpy start I had almost thirty years ago. My only wish is that it had happened sooner. That is why this book is my way of passing the baton to all of you readers, to ensure that you have a shorter path to success with the help of the following pages.

Happy reading!

# Chapter 1

## Why I'm Not a Pilot

### *Lessons From My Childhood Dreams*

*"Failure is a part of the process. You just learn to pick yourself back up." – Michelle Obama*

It took me a long time to realise that just because you want something from the core of your being doesn't mean you're going to get it. That's not how life works. All that talk about wanting something and the universe conspiring to help you achieve it is, I believe, wishful thinking. If that were the case, I'd be flying fighter jets right now.

Growing up, I wanted to be a fighter pilot for the Indian Air Force. It consumed my every thought since I was six years old, and I made every decision—whether it was subjects to focus on in school or the right sport to pursue—keeping that goal in mind. If there was a way to achieve your dream just by wanting it badly enough, I would have had a completely different life.

I know now that the reason my work desk isn't a cockpit is because I didn't give my hundred per cent when I had the chance. Instead, I blamed destiny and bad luck and cursed the powers that be for leaving me in a state I was completely unprepared for. What was I going to do with my life if I couldn't be a fighter pilot?

Well, I figured it out. Along the way, I learnt a few things. Hence, this book. These lessons and what you take away from them can make a difference between finding success sooner and waiting for your turn as life moves along.

## Lesson #1: You Have To Throw Everything But The Kitchen Sink At It

When I was a kid, I talked about flying all the time. My father joined the Indian Air Force (IAF) as a Junior Commissioned Officer and retired as a Master Warrant Officer who specialised in the launch of surface-to-air missiles. I grew up around fighter pilots and would imitate how they walked and talked. My bedroom walls were plastered with the fifteen Officer-Like Qualities (OLQs) that armed forces officers swore by. OLQs are the core attributes that define a candidate's potential as an officer in the armed forces. Even now, almost thirty years later, I still remember them all:

| Factor I – Planning & Organisation | Factor II – Social Adjustment | Factor III – Social Effectiveness | Factor IV – Dynamic |
| --- | --- | --- | --- |
| Effective Intelligence | Social Adaptability | Initiative | Determination |
| Reasoning Ability | Cooperation | Self-Confidence | Courage |
| Organisational Ability | Sense of Responsibility | Speed of Decision | Stamina |
| Power of Expression | Ability to Influence Groups | Liveliness | |

I believed I had imbibed all these qualities and studied like a man possessed to clear the Union Public Service Commission (UPSC) exam for the Combined Defence Services Examination (CDSE).

The day I passed it you'd have struggled to find a happier kid. Next up were the personality and physical tests, which is where I messed up.

Before I tell you where I went wrong, let me first mention what happens at the interview stage. Once an armed forces candidate clears the written exams, the Ministry of Defence assigns them to a location for the interview phase of the Service Selection Board (SSB). You're locked there for five days and first tested for leadership skills at a group discussion. Then follow the physical strength tests and command tasks. Next, the candidate has to go through a psychological test to assess how you would react to different situations of danger and conflict. On the last day is an interview. At the end of this five-day process, the final results are declared. Those selected are asked to stay back, and the rest are ushered into a bus and dropped at the nearest train station.

No points for guessing which camp I belonged to. The first time I failed was in Mysore. The train journey from down south to Delhi was long and heartbreaking. The overwhelming feeling was disbelief. How could I, who had wanted this so badly, have failed? I had passed the written exam, so what could have gone wrong?

I wasn't one to give up easily, so I attempted the whole routine again. This time, too, the written exam was an easier task. But at the end of the five days of physical and mental tests in Varanasi, the result was the same. I had failed again.

A few months later, it was time for attempt #3. I headed to Bhopal, determined to pass the second phase of the exam. There was no way God would fail me again, right? I was wrong. I was sent back home again with nothing to show for all the years I put in preparing for what I thought was the role of a lifetime.

I had failed three times now. The writing was on the wall; it was time to give up. The flying dream was over.

The Ministry of Defence doesn't tell you why you've failed – something that needs to be corrected immediately. And I, blinded by self-righteousness, couldn't figure out until years later why I wasn't among the chosen ones to fly a jet for the Indian Air Force.

What I didn't know then was that there was no way I would have passed. I was an introvert who rarely took initiative. My shyness stopped me from engaging with people. I had spent all my time and effort trying to ace the written exam and none on enhancing my personality. I bitterly regret that. Had I done so, I'm sure my dream would have come true.

I was surrounded by fighter pilots as a youngster; they were all roaming around my father's place of work, and I had access to them all the time. I should have taken the first step and spoken to a few of them about what I needed to do to become like them. I should have asked questions like: How did you get in? What kind of prep did you do? What are the key areas I should focus on? I could have asked them or my siblings to practise speaking in front of a group with me. I should have networked. But I didn't think all this was important. The armed forces aren't just looking for officers; they want commanders and future leaders on their roster. I didn't develop my personality to suit their needs. I had my own assumptions of what was required to become a pilot, and I refused to see if there was anything else I was missing out on.

My big lesson from my failure to make my childhood dream a reality is that I should have given it my all. I should have consulted people whose careers I wanted to emulate instead of depending on unreliable sources. I should have prepared myself thoroughly and not been restricted by what I thought was enough. I hope you, the readers, can learn from this and not repeat my goof-ups.

## Lesson #2: Say No When You Want To

The reason I was shy and introverted was that growing up we were all taught that saying no means disobedience. Children who said no were undisciplined and needed to be pulled up. So, saying no was a no-no, and it took me a long time to unlearn this ridiculous lesson.

When I didn't qualify for the armed forces, I had to rethink the entire trajectory of my life. Unfortunately, there was no lightbulb moment, like in the movies, where there was sudden redemption, and I ended up with a dream career the next day. That sure footing came after years of drifting around.

A couple of months after my third rejection from the Ministry of Defence, I was reading the newspaper at home. In those days, the Times of India used to have an Ascent supplement that advertised jobs. The National Institute of Information Technology (NIIT) was looking for graphic designers, and the open call for interviewees was scheduled for that same day. I quickly changed, borrowed my father's scooter, and left. At no time did I pause to think that I knew absolutely nothing about graphic design.

Despite having no experience or qualifications in graphic design, I ended up at NIIT's office in Kalkaji, New Delhi for over twelve hours. I struggled through the tests but still found myself going through the various selection phases. At the end of a long day, the HR person told me it was a very tough call. That I was just an arts graduate, that I didn't have an advanced diploma from any computer institute, and that I was not even computer-literate. Despite all my shortcomings, they decided to offer me the job. But because of my shortcomings, they could only pay me INR 3,200 a month.

I was so consumed with desperation and thoughts of the IAF rejection looming in my mind that I didn't hesitate before accepting her offer, a designation that was one above a janitor in that company.

What an idiot I was!

In hindsight, even though that was my first time doing anything related to graphic design, I had clearly done a good job. Why else would NIIT offer me the job? No organisation hires a person they think is unfit for the role. Despite my complete lack of experience, I must have impressed them enough to be offered the job. If I had realised this that day, if I had known my worth, I would have said a resounding no to the HR person.

I would have said, 'No, you need to pay me more than what you're offering.'

Had I said so, she would have agreed to pay me the salary I wanted and deserved. I didn't understand the power of 'no'. When used wisely, 'no' shows that you value yourself, your time, and your efforts. It stops you from getting exploited. It takes courage to say 'no'. A 'no' is rarely received well. But when you say 'no' to set limits, it sets you free. You can then negotiate better deals for yourself. Saying 'no' shows that you prioritise yourself and choose the options that suit you best.

## Lesson #3: Goal >> Vision >> Action Plan

Some things are very simple: Without a goal, you're unlikely to get much success. And visualising your goal will help you create the pathway for it. You can work backwards and pave your path towards what needs to be done to get there. Say, for instance, that you want to become a professional football player. Only when you dream of playing for a club or your country can you plan the roadmap to reach there.

But just dreaming about something or having a wishlist isn't enough. You need a very detailed action plan that is time-bound. A common mistake we all make is that we have plans but we don't give ourselves a deadline to execute them. Without deadlines, we humans are bound to falter. We will procrastinate and waste precious time.

So, a clear-cut vision and a clear-cut plan with a deadline that you follow with self-discipline and total honesty will get you what you want.

This rule applies to anyone pursuing a career in a field of their choice. Whenever I'm mentoring someone, the first thing I tell them is to close their eyes and visualise what their dream life looks like. Forget about your life right now and imagine it when you have retired. Maybe you want to live in a bungalow surrounded by mountains and streams. Maybe you're sipping cocktails on the beach and swimming in the ocean. Or you see awards for your excellent work lined up on your living room wall. That's your end state; your goal.

Once you know where you see yourself at the end of your working life, identify your icons or role models. Research them and their lives. What was that person's background? What did he/she do? How does that person carry themselves? How do they dress, walk, and talk? You need to understand all this so that you can emulate them. The same acts always result in the same output. So if you follow the life of your role models, you are more or less likely to reach where they are.

When I started working with NIIT as a graphic designer, there was one thing I always looked forward to: an email in my inbox every Monday. Some colleagues would have returned from the USA after their project and sent a mass email telling us all about Hershey's Kisses chocolates at their desks. These guys would be dressed in business casual attire: Allen Solly shirt and trousers and Woodland shoes. Even though the clothes and shoes were bought in India, I wanted to be like them.

While eating those US-return chocolates, I would dream about being in the USA and living my life there. I started watching Hollywood movies even though I struggled to understand the accent. I started painting a mental picture of the USA. I also began to observe the people who returned from there after their projects. What skill sets did they have? What did they do there? After talking to some of them casually at the coffee vending machine, I figured out that I need to develop some technical skills if I want to be considered for a project that would take me to the USA.

Luckily, the opportunity came knocking when, due to a quality issue in some of our products, we had to redevelop them and fix the bugs quickly. For the work to be more effective, everyone was given technical training related to their products. I grabbed this break, signed up for the training, and completed my Microsoft Certified System Engineer (MCSE) certification. This certification gave me a monthly special skill allowance. And what did I do with it? I bought my first pair of Allen Solly shirt and trousers and Woodland shoes!

I had a goal, and I worked on a vision plan, and looked out for role models whom I could emulate.

I mentioned earlier that I joined NIIT at the lowest possible position. A couple of months in, I couldn't wait to come out of that salary bracket and better my financial prospects. I was extremely embarrassed that from being on course to becoming a fighter pilot, I was earning a pittance. That's when I started reinvesting in my career. The MCSE certifications led me to become the only such engineer in my department. That's how I created opportunities that became a ladder to take me to my final destination, the United States of America.

As always, this was in no way a simple matter, and I'll speak more about this in a later chapter.

## Lesson #4: Pivot

When something isn't working for you, it is best to find a new course. It works in every aspect of life, be it relationships, finances, or your career. When your heart isn't in a project, that's a big sign that it's not meant for you.

An excellent example would be of my nephew. About eight or nine years ago, I visited India for work and had dinner with him. He was studying for a BTech degree at a private university in Noida. The talk veered to his studies, and he shared that he wasn't really interested in becoming an engineer. His heart wasn't in it. He did like the world of finance and investing but saw no way to pursue that. He was considering dropping out and figuring out the future. That was not a wise move, and I convinced him to change his mind. The correct thing to do would be to gain additional skills in the field he was interested in while completing his graduation.

He was spending eight to ten hours in college, with the rest of the time hanging out with friends. I suggested that he spend a few of his free hours exploring finance and investing as a career. Investing based on insider tips and playing the guessing game was utterly foolish and could have devastating results. What he needed to learn was the science behind how the share market works.

Since his parents were funding his life, they wouldn't allow him to change course. So step one was to gain financial independence. I recommended that he read some books that would be helpful. *Rich Dad Poor Dad* because it's a great book about honing your financial acumen, *Who Moved My Cheese?* for change and adaptability, and then *The Peter Principle* for unavoidable incompetency in the workplace.

I'm glad he took my advice seriously. The books must have had an impact because one day I received a call from his father who told me that his son had come home from our talk excited about his future and that he had started investing in the stock market as a side hustle. He had also completed some National Stock Exchange and Bombay Stock Exchange certifications, which gave him the skills and insights required to do well as a stock trader. That turned out to be a masterstroke and now he's doing great. He's become a successful financial consultant and is earning a tidy fortune every month. Isn't it wonderful when, with a bit of nip and tuck, life works out? The right advice at the right time can truly change your life. And I'm thrilled that I played a small part in it.

The takeaway from my nephew's story is that it's never too late to pivot towards your passion. Recognise the dissatisfaction you're currently feeling and don't let it overwhelm you. It may seem like there is no way out. But life is a long journey, and everyone will eventually find their way to career and financial happiness. You just have to be smart about it.

Another person I recently mentored had a similar story. I lost my mother in 2023 and on my last day in India, one of my aunts asked me to speak with her grandson. I had observed this boy the last few days. He and his mobile phone were constant companions. You wouldn't see one without the other. He would spend at least a couple of hours of his day lounging on the terrace, lost in his phone. We got to talking as I packed my bags, and he told me that he was studying biology. I don't meet a lot of young people studying this subject, so I asked him why biology interested him. Turns out, it didn't. He had no idea what he wanted to study after school. When his mother suggested biology, he must have shrugged his shoulders and obeyed. And now he had no interest in studying and not much hope for his future either.

This is what happens when you are meandering through life without knowing your destination. Anything done half-heartedly is a waste of precious time – time that can be utilised doing something that makes every day a joy.

I gave him the same spiel I gave my nephew and it turns out he too was interested in a career in investing and finance. I recommended that he read the same books. I clearly must have hit a nerve in our conversation because a day after I reached home, he sent me a WhatsApp message with a picture of the books he had bought. It was lovely to read his message. Now he's started investing his pocket money, and as part of his regular communication with me, he told me his success rate is about 70 per cent. He's still a young kid trying to find his way in the world, but he is no longer that directionless adolescent who wasted hours of his day.

It gladdens my heart to see young people like him benefit from my experiences. To know that I have changed the course of someone's life is an immense responsibility and one I don't take lightly. These are talks I wish someone had had with me. We all learn from our own mistakes – hopefully. But if we can learn from other people's foibles, we can avoid all their heartbreaking experiences and moments of pain. I couldn't do that. But I wish you can, from mine.

# Chapter 2

# I Failed Again, and Again, and Again

## *What Repeated Rejections Taught Me*

*"Failure should be our teacher, not our undertaker. Failure is delay, not defeat. It is a temporary detour, not a dead end. Failure is something we can avoid only by saying nothing, doing nothing, and being nothing." – Denis Waitley*

Do you know about the ninety-day rule when a relationship ends? It says that you should give yourself at least three months to process a break-up; this time can help you grow, heal, and think about yourself and your needs. That rule should apply to other aspects of life too, giving us time to lick our wounds and bid a fitting farewell to the death of our dreams.

Life, unfortunately, isn't always that kind. At twenty, when my dream of becoming a fighter pilot had gone up in smoke, I was suddenly thrown from my cocoon into the big, bad world. I now had to swim without a life jacket and figure out what to do for the rest of my life. So I did a bit of what the kids now call 'adulting' and redefined my idea of success. I now aspired to work in a job that paid me well, gave me independence, and where I was treated with dignity and respect.

Success means different things to all of us. It also changes at different stages of life. But the means to achieve it remain the same for everyone. No matter your end goal, the effort you put in and the rules you follow to reach it don't change. In this chapter, I will speak about the secrets of success that have worked for me.

## Lesson #1: Self-discipline

Self-discipline is the bedrock upon which empires are built, dreams are realised, and destinies are shaped. In my experience, self-discipline is not about doing the things you need to do; it is about not doing things that you are not supposed to do. The enemy of self-discipline is temptation. The more you try to resist something, the more time you will spend thinking about it. The mental and physical fight to resist temptation will tell you how self-disciplined you are.

It is self-discipline that ensured I passed the written UPSC test. I may not have crossed the second hurdle of clearing the SSB physical and social skills evaluation exam, but it was self-discipline that took me that far. I was most definitely not the smartest person there. But I put in the hours I felt were necessary, and it paid off. The most difficult part of self-discipline is time management. If you can learn to manage your time effectively, everything else will fall into place and the success you desire will be yours for the taking.

I don't know how or why I was that way, but I taught myself to be self-disciplined since childhood. Growing up in a family that was a part of the Indian armed forces surely helped. There's a reason why army, navy, and air force personnel live a regimented lifestyle. All that discipline equips them to lead an optimum life. They are ready to face all sorts of challenges at any time. So when I was a teenager, I kept timetables for everything, which included slots for exercise, study time, mealtime, and when I would relax. It's a habit I have carried forward to this day.

Time management will help you stick to your plan. And then the plan will help you stick to the task that's required. I've realised that if a person can just focus on time or develop self-discipline around time management, it will take them towards success.

## Lesson #2: God Has A Purpose For All Of Us, So Don't Settle

God is not the same for everyone. For you, it may be an all-knowing being that's above humans. Or you call God 'fate' or 'universe'. Regardless of how you describe the entity, I have realised that God has something planned for all of us. That plan, as we all know, is unlikely to reveal itself on demand. But it will eventually come to you. In the meantime, you have to give life your best.

After giving my fighter pilot dream three shots, I finally accepted that I was definitely not sent to Earth for that purpose. In the next few months of despair, when I didn't know what would become of me, I considered following the path of my father and brother. The Indian armed forces accept candidates at two levels. Anyone who has passed class 12 or its equivalent diploma is eligible for a junior entry-level job of airmen. It entails a much simpler entrance exam when compared to the UPSC test. But for commissioned officers, they are looking out for officers who possess the fifteen OLQs I mentioned in the previous chapter—hence the rigorous UPSC test. My father and brother had both joined as airmen. Training to be a commissioned officer, I had learnt skills like flying, horse-riding, and shooting—things that could not be used in any other career. *So why not go into the family endeavour*, I had thought.

I appeared for the airmen test, and, years later, I would remember the result of it every time I watched an episode of the game show that actor Shah Rukh Khan hosted, *Kya Aap Paanchvi Paas Se Tez Hai?* or

AKA *Are You Smarter than a 5th Grader?*. On the show, adults who had obviously passed school and now had successful careers were tested on their class 5 knowledge. It was hilarious to watch them stumble over questions they had mastered as schoolchildren. That's who I was the day the results of the airmen entrance exam were announced. A person who had passed the extremely difficult UPSC written exam three times had failed a much easier exam, something that I could have attempted in my sleep. If this were a WhatsApp message, a facepalm emoji would have followed.

Thankfully, I was no longer the desperate person who had attempted this exam a few months ago. I had calmed down mentally. It didn't take me much time to bounce back because I knew that God didn't want me to settle for less than what I wanted and what I was capable of. He had better plans for me. I just had to continue to find my true purpose and keep looking ahead. Well, that's what I did, and my life turned out to be better than I had expected.

## Lesson #3: Few Things Are More Important Than Financial Freedom

In 2019, a lovely movie called *Super 30* was released, about a teacher from Bihar who trained thirty underprivileged young men and women for the super difficult entrance exams to the IITs. I, with family roots in Bihar, had my own version of the film going on at my house when I was only sixteen years old. Only mine would have been called Super 4, and the kids I was teaching were in school.

Someday that movie may also be made, but for now, I'm glad that it set me on the path to financial independence, one that I have always cherished and been proud of. I took on those kids because I was known as a bright student in my neighbourhood and their parents wanted me to tutor them after school. I taught them all subjects. I decided to take up the parents' offer because I wanted to earn some money to supplement my education. My father had been paying my college fees, and I wanted to take care of the rest. But I also knew even then that money has an irresistible attraction. That's another place where self-discipline helped me immensely. So just the four kids paying me INR 200 each was enough.

Other than the financial benefit, teaching them also helped me revise my knowledge for the CDSE exam. With the money, I bought copies of magazines, newspapers, and periodicals to prepare for my exam. I reinvested the money in my education. I didn't use it for any other needs, not even to purchase water. In those days, in the scorching Delhi summer heat, water would be sold for 25 paise a glass. I would get thirsty but didn't want to spend the money on anything other than what was required for my exam prep.

This way, I avoided the hesitant feeling I got when I had to ask my father for any additional financial help. I was partly responsible for myself, and it was a great feeling. Of course, my father would have been happy to pay for anything I needed, but I didn't want him to do that.

This kind of financial freedom gives you a lot of room to make decisions about your own life. You aren't under anyone's control. Money gives you the power and strength to say no whenever you want, and that's something every single person should feel. Money means empowerment and choices. Only a foolish person would deny themselves that.

## Lesson #4: Learn and learn. You never know where it will take you.

I mentioned in the previous chapter that I was hired as a graphic designer and visualiser at NIIT. My team and I designed courses on

Transmission Control Protocol/Internet Protocol that prospective learners could purchase in the form of CDs at bookstores like Barnes and Noble in the US. Our technical team would write the script, and it was my job to visualise it to make it fun for the student. They would install them on their computers and learn on their own. Clearly, e-learning has been around for much longer than current start-ups would like us to believe.

One day, we were told that sixty of those courses had errors in them and had to be immediately withdrawn from the market. Those titles had to be changed. We faced a lot of issues, but we completed the task on time. Interestingly, we had nicknamed this project QE2, named after the ship Queen Elizabeth 2, which was made right after the Titanic. We were determined to ensure that ours wouldn't sink like the infamous unsinkable one, and we were right.

After the dust had settled and we could take a breather, we were all called for a meeting with the leadership team to discuss what we could learn from this fiasco. By then, I had spent a few months at NIIT and felt confident to voice my opinion. I told the room that graphic designers like me should be given technical knowledge too. After all, we were the ones who made the drab mechanical script fun and interesting. If we knew how the software worked, we'd be able to do our jobs better. I'm so glad I did that because it served as the foundation for everything that was to come next in my career.

The leadership team agreed, but graphic designers would be considered for the project only if we passed a test after the technical training course was completed. I, as usual, gave it my all and was excited to learn something new. This made the exam a breeze. Even then, I was shocked to learn that I had topped it. Of the ten others who had appeared for it, I was the only one who was computer-illiterate and had no technical or engineering degree. I was ecstatic and my manager was impressed.

I worked on a few more projects which gave me a lot of creative satisfaction. I was backing up one of my projects one day when I was struck by a simple thing. As you know, when any file transfers from one folder to another, it flies from one to the other. It took me a moment to realise what a perfect representation that was of a file transfer. On the backend, it's 0s and 1s doing the work, but what the user sees on the screen has been designed by a graphic designer like me. It took me a while, but I was at last fascinated by my job.

So I wanted to know if I could teach myself based on the graphics and visuals I had created for a course. I installed the course on my computer and started learning with the help of my graphics. Surprisingly, it was easier than I thought! I learnt it quickly. When I told my colleague and friend, Santosh Soni, about it, he quietly did something that I was aghast at then but turned out to be one of the best things to ever happen to me.

He paid INR 850 and enrolled me for a Microsoft Certified System Engineer Certification programme called Windows NT 4.0 TCP/IP. So far I had only been tinkering around with computers and didn't take them seriously as a profession. This certification was way out of my league. But my friend was adamant that I should appear. I did and, once again to my surprise, I scored 900 out of 1,000 marks. Who would have ever thought that I, who had landed at NIIT by chance, was performing so well? After that, as I had promised to my friend, I appeared for five more tests for the same certification. Even as I was doing all these incredible things, I was aware that something remarkable was going to come of this. These were tough tests to pass, and I was approximately the 35,000[th] person in the world to get that certificate.

I had an extremely supportive manager who believed in my potential. He wanted me promoted and did all the behind-the-scenes work to make that happen. In fact, he wrote an email that I was instructed to copy and send to him, which he would forward to our superiors. Because of that email, I was promoted to the technical department. That's how my journey in tech began.

And it was all thanks to my eagerness to learn something new. I was curious even when I wasn't sure I was interested in the subject. It just goes to show that we never know where life takes us. All we can do is keep an open mind and soak in as much as we can. That, along with a few benefactors along the way, paid off handsomely.

## Lesson #5: Don't Look Back; There's Nothing There

Have you realised that when something good happens in your life, you immediately start thinking of the next good thing that will occur? Once I got the systems administrator role at NIIT, I felt that something better was just around the corner for me. So I started looking at international opportunities. Those Monday morning chocolates planted the seed of an American dream in my mind, and I was exploring avenues that would help me make the move abroad.

I soon got an interview call with a company called PayPal. Nobody knew PayPal then, but we all know it now as Elon Musk's second start-up. Musk co-founded X.com, a direct bank. X.com merged with Confinity in 2000 to form PayPal. I must have done well to get offered the job and a salary of USD 55,000. I had never dreamt of so much money and I took a couple of minutes to check if the zeros were correct. And now the daydreams started. Whenever I closed my eyes, I could see a Mitsubishi Pajero—the hottest car of that time— in front of me. I also knew the colours it would have: white with a red door. Nothing could stop me now. I was going to the US, send dollars home, and my parents could start building a mansion.

Since the offer letter had come in, I went to my hometown, Muzaffarpur in Bihar, where we had a family reunion. While my family was excited about my career prospects, they were worried that I would lose my way in a foreign land. I hadn't quit my job at NIIT because the visa papers from PayPal had yet to arrive. I faced some family pressure to quit and spend that time at home. So I did, which wasn't the brightest decision I've made in life.

At that time, my parents had retired to Muzaffarpur and I was staying alone in Delhi. So I used my NIIT office address for all correspondence. So, when the visa papers were sent to NIIT, I wasn't there to receive them. I believed that the courier package would come to me, forgetting that the address was different. When it was pretty close to my date of travel, the recruiter asked me when my visa interview was scheduled. But I had questions of my own for him – why hadn't I received the papers? Turns out, they were sent to me, but to the NIIT address. My heart was in my mouth at this time. I rushed to the office and found the delivery noted in the guard's register. But no one could locate where it was. I knew who had messed around with it. There were a couple of colleagues who were in a technical role for ten to twelve years, and they didn't like how I had been promoted and I already had a foreign job offer at this young age. But I couldn't do anything about it.

The American dream was over. There would be nothing for me at PayPal, and I could see the Pajero vanishing before me. And I had quit my job at NIIT. The simplest option would have been to call my manager and request him to reconsider me for that job. I was even advised to do that. But I don't like to look back. It's the past and should remain there. Going back to that job would mean going back in life. I needed to move forward. I was adamant that that wasn't the correct trajectory for me, and I trusted my skills enough to back up my claims.

I was back on the job market and within a couple of weeks, I landed a manager's role with a privately held capital investment company in Delhi. I did so well there that I was offered a bonus even before my first year was over. That had never happened in that company before. I wouldn't have gotten that if I hadn't done the unexpected.

We all come across many such moments in life when choosing the comfortable option seems like the right one. But no change can come from comfort. We need to be out there testing ourselves against the elements to know what we're truly made of. And once you take that chance and don't look back, a world of possibilities opens up.

## Lesson #6: The Decision You Make In Any Circumstance Is The Best One At That Time

I was enjoying my time at the investment firm because I had turned many things around there. My proudest moment came when I saved the company INR 35 lakhs in penalties to Microsoft by moving them to another platform. That was a huge deal, and my efforts had been appreciated.

One day, though, I overheard a colleague talking about a recent Microsoft software purchase that we had made, worth around INR 4 lakhs. And that my team and I must have received kickbacks for it. Those furious animals we see in cartoons, the ones who go redder with each passing second, that was me. I went up to my colleague and yelled at him like I had never done with anyone before. I had never taken a rupee that wasn't mine, and now someone was accusing me of stealing profits!

I immediately went to my office, typed out a resignation letter, sent it to my manager, and walked out. There were a lot of apology calls in the next few days, but I was not going to budge from my decision. Once again, as I was reaching the top of my performance, I was hit by another setback, and I was jobless again.

This is, however, just the set-up until I reach the important part of the story – what I learnt from it. Many people called my decision to quit based on an accusation—that they took back and apologised for—reckless. And maybe it was. But it gave me the momentum to move forward. Everything turned out well, so I don't regret it.

You may think: it's easy to not regret things in hindsight because it ultimately worked out for me. But they may not have worked out as well. To be completely honest, I never regretted my decision to quit, even at that time. I was in my late twenties, and maybe it was my youth telling me that I control the world and no one can stop me.

Something I have always learnt and relearnt in life is that when you make any decision, it is the best decision that you made at that time, in that circumstance. Only time will tell whether it is right or wrong. But, in that particular moment, everyone only takes the decision they believe is the right one. Some people go with their instincts at such times. Others, even though they make it emotionally, definitely evaluate some options.

Regardless of the reasons, it's the best decision that your mind comes up with. So, there is no point in repenting it later if it doesn't turn in your favour. You have to tell yourself that it's a done deal; it's the locked answer on *Kaun Banega Crorepati*, AKA *Who Wants to be a Millionaire*. Just keep moving on and see what you can do next. It's better to course-correct than to think about it and wish you had not done that.

Maybe this is how I am because of all the OLQ trainings that were a part of my moral fibre. Growing up, in my mind, I was already a fighter pilot. It's how I'd wired myself since childhood. Fighter pilots fly solo. They are on their own in the cockpit flying at twice the speed of sound. I had always told myself that I am the one who'll be taking decisions for the INR 200-crore plane I would be sitting in. So only I was responsible for all my decisions, good or bad.

That's what I must have thought too when I made the decision to just up and leave. I never discussed it with my parents, siblings, or friends. And I was all right about that. I'd trained myself to take charge of my life, and this is how I was doing it.

I was going to take this flight to the runway myself.

# Chapter 3

# The Shifting Goalpost



## _Keeping Up With Changing Circumstances_

_"In order to design a future of positive change, we must first become experts at changing our minds." – Jacque Fresco_

I love the Hindi word for a shameless person. Besharam. It's a word that's often used in Indian society to describe someone who doesn't fit the norm, who dances to the tune of their own beat, who doesn't give a damn. Besharam people are judged for the choices they make, for defying the unwritten codes of society.

But well-behaved people rarely make history. I'm proof of that. I didn't change the fortunes of a country. Nor did I come up with a path-breaking invention. But I changed the course of my own life. I pulled myself up by the bootstraps and created a life for myself that was beyond the expectations of anyone who knew me years ago. And I did that by being besharam.

### Lesson #1: Be Shameless!

Many years ago, I saw a show on TV where former cricketer Navjot Singh Sidhu was talking about his achievements. One thing he said stuck with me: Duniya ka sabse bada rog, kya kahenge log. The biggest disease the world suffers from is worrying about what other people will think. It was an incredible insight into why so many people are held back from living their full lives. They think about other people's reactions to their actions and self-correct to avoid any friction. And, in the process, they live stunted lives, rarely realising their full potential.

I, thankfully, was one of the shameless ones. I did what I thought was right for me at every step of the way, and it has led me to the successful life I'm living today.

If you recall, I had left a managerial position at an investment firm because I was accused of receiving kickbacks. I refused to go back even after they admitted to making a mistake and pleaded with me to come back. I can never accept anyone questioning my integrity. So I found myself jobless once again. One day, while driving past a street, I saw a recruitment ad for a job at a call centre that was a part of Compaq's technical support. I didn't have a job then, so why not give this a try? A job at a call centre answering customer questions in an American accent would have been humiliating for someone else. I was, after all, a Microsoft-certified engineer, one of only 35,000 in the world. And here I was competing with undergraduates, who wanted to work at the call centre for pocket money.

Taking a job that is below your skills can be embarrassing, especially since people identify themselves based on the work they do. Yes, sitting in that room with people who weren't half as qualified as me and seeking the same job as them could have been shameful for me. But I never thought of walking out. I was actively seeking my purpose in life and wanted to know if this was the place that would give me career fulfilment. Turns out, I was overqualified for it because I scored 100 per cent in both the language as well as the computer skills test. In fact, the interviewers thought this was my second or third attempt since I knew the answers to all the questions.

After I convinced them that this was the first time I had entered their office, I was hired. I had a job and I was ecstatic about it. I went through a month of process as well as voice and accent training. I already knew the technical aspects of the job because of my Microsoft certification. But the accent training was a bit of a task. I was extremely nervous as I answered my first call. I had never spoken to an American person before. Would they know I wasn't Ronald but plain ol' Rakesh? What if they were unhappy with the support I was supposed to provide them? I was in the midst of the first call when someone tapped me on the shoulder, asked me to disconnect the call, and meet the vice president of operations in the conference room immediately.

*There goes one more job*, was my first thought. Turns out, my trainer, who was also my manager, had quit that day, and I was being asked to fill his position. What did I just hear? I was being promoted to a trainer's position on the first day of my job? My manager had recommended my name because he thought I had done a good job during the training process. I had to start that evening at 2 a.m.

I worked there for four to five months, but I quit soon for a couple of reasons. I had condensed the 200-page training manual to just 30 pages because much of the information wasn't relevant. Since my trainees were performing better than those who were stuck with the original manual, my peers didn't like me. My former colleague at NIIT invited me to join him in his entrepreneurial venture in e-learning.

I was ready to move on by then because I had done everything I could have at the call centre. I wasn't going to go any higher up the ranks. The call centre job taught me the importance of not feeling any kind of shame. All jobs deserve respect. If I had felt shame, I wouldn't have been able to step into that call centre. If I hadn't learnt to be shameless, I'd have missed out on the confidence boost for acing the interview and getting promoted on day one. It's important to remember that sometimes you may have to take up something that wasn't in your plan. But you improvise, you learn, and you move forward.

## Lesson #2: Don't Let Anyone Take You For Granted

Before my stint at the call centre, I worked at a computer training institute in Delhi. The Microsoft certification had given me one-of-a-kind skills, and there was plenty of demand for people who could teach others that. I was hired instantly and started teaching. A month later, when my salary was due, nothing was reflected in my bank account. One more week went by, and still nothing.

I spoke to a colleague who told me the whole team had not been paid for the last seven months! How was that even possible? Why were these people working there for free? I spoke to the vice president who dismissed me by saying that I wasn't special and that I would be paid along with the others. Now I was outraged. It didn't matter how the company treated others, but I needed my salary yesterday.

Since this was a Singapore-based company, I wrote an email to one of the higher-ups there and informed them about the goings-on at their office in India. I'm glad I did so because three days later, I was paid all my dues. And the moment it reflected in my bank account, I submitted my resignation. I did not want to work in a company that did not respect the work of its employees. We are all here to be gainfully employed and earn money that can sustain our lifestyle. A company that doesn't understand that is not worth your time.

Once again, even though I didn't have a job lined up, I wasn't going to allow a company to take me or my time for granted.

However, I took care of the seven students I was teaching. I couldn't abandon them midway. So even though I had quit, I met them outside the institute every evening and answered all of their questions. I also helped them with the registration process. My friend had done that for me once, and I was passing that good luck along. All seven students got their certification and are doing well now. And I'm happy to have done that.

## Lesson #3: Respond To Opportunities Positively

A lot of what I write in this book can happen only with a shift in mindset. There is a lot of advice out there, most of which is actually helpful. But unless you change the way your mind processes experiences, the trajectory of your life isn't going to change much. A large part of grabbing what's in front of you is recognising that it is an opportunity in the first place. And the beautiful part about life is that most things that happen to us *are* opportunities. We are all guilty of overthinking and finding reasons for not doing something, rather than opening ourselves to the possibility that it can turn out even better than expected. You have to actively work towards developing the courage to accept the risk that comes with an opportunity. Only two things can happen when you do so. Either you will be successful or you will learn something new. Because I don't believe there is anything called failure.

I know many people say that. When I was young and I would hear someone older say that, I'd end up feeling angry. But as I grew up and saw all the different aspects of life, I can tell you that people who say that failure doesn't exist are right. That's why I wasn't scared of experimenting. The only skills that I had growing up were flying planes, horse-riding, and shooting. They were pretty useless in the real world. So the only way I could learn something marketable was to soak in as much as I could. That's why I was a graphic designer, teacher, trainer, and manager in vastly different industries before finding what I was meant to do.

Let me tell you a secret. When a potential opportunity presents itself, don't ask, 'What's in it for me?' Instead, tell yourself, 'There is definitely something in it for me. Maybe that is why God has put me on this path.' Once you do that, the fear of the unknown will dissipate.

## Lesson #4: Reject Everything You Don't Want To Do

We always know what is right for us. We may not be able to explain why we feel that way, but our gut instinct always points us in the correct direction. The trick is learning to reject what we feel isn't working for us. The ability to say no cannot be gained overnight. The only way to hone it is to use it as much as possible. When you accept the power that saying no gives you, nothing will stand in your path anymore.

Let me illustrate that with an example. I left the call centre trainer job because my former colleague from NIIT had invited me to join him in starting a business venture. As always, I was ready for the next adventure and I agreed to his proposition. Our company, Digital Interactive Media Solution, developed self-learning content for publishing houses like McGraw Hill who, in turn, sold it to international schools. We were successful, and there was no need to pivot from our core business. But I wanted more. I wanted to bring the power of IT into India's education system. In the early 2000s, there were barely any e-learning platforms which are ubiquitous these days. I wanted Indian institutions to embrace the 'direct instruction' methodology of education, wherein you sign up for an online course and learn from the teacher who is present on the screen, who is, essentially, speaking only to you. I was so convinced by the idea that I wrote to the president of India, Dr A. P. J. Abdul Kalam, asking for his intervention. I also wrote to industrialist Subroto Roy because he had spoken about building smart cities. And what was smarter than e-learning?

My partner did not approve of me pushing my own agenda and trying to take our company in a direction he was not comfortable with. But I was determined to see where this could lead me, and I told him that I would do what I believed was right for me, for our business, and for the Indian education system.

Our teaching methodologies needed an overhaul. According to Siegfried Engelmann and Wesley Becker, the direct instruction methodology consisted of about seven steps: 1) objectives, 2) standards, 3) anticipatory set, 4) teaching (input, modelling, and check for understanding), 5) guided practice, 6) closure, and 7) independent practice. I was so impressed with this methodology that I spoke to officials from Delhi's top public schools and international schools about adopting it and letting our company help them.

Unfortunately, all my efforts were in vain. Nobody wanted to disrupt the existing system and invest in challenging the status quo. I was also unable to get someone to sponsor INR 1.5 lakh to bring the Engelmann and Becker scheme to India to coach teachers in direct instruction here.

I have no regrets because I did not fail. I was able to explore this nascent industry—one that millions of children in India are now taking advantage of—and educate myself about it.

There's one more incident that reinforced the thought that you have to put your foot down if you are unhappy with something. Only then will your circumstances change for the better.

Years later, when I was working for Wipro Technologies, we worked on several projects for Microsoft. I was an arts graduate. I was initially a science student who shifted to commerce. And when I failed in my first year of commerce college, I moved to arts. I was an outlier at a tech company where all my peers were BTech and BE graduates. I always fit in despite my different educational background because I had taught myself all the technical requirements to get the job at Wipro. However, I realised I was being treated differently because my colleagues were being sent to the US for short-term projects and I wasn't.

I was told that they couldn't put my name forward for visa processing because the minimum requirement for that was graduation in science. That was ridiculous! I was working the night shift that day and before it began at 1.30 a.m., I called my boss. I was shameless in my conversation with him. I told him that I wanted to resign because my work wasn't being respected. If an arts graduate was good enough to be working on the same projects and teams as science graduates, he was definitely good enough for foreign assignments. I did my everyday job exactly like my colleagues. There was no discrimination in the work we were assigned. So why the different attitude towards me? Thankfully, I had a good boss who heard me out even at that late hour. He told me to wait till the end of my shift. When it ended at 6.30 a.m., I was surprised to see my boss walk into the office in his tracksuit. What followed was a great conversation over a cup of tea where he told me that he completely understood my point of view. He had thought of a way for me to get what I was seeking. He had observed that I was exceptional at building relationships and interacting with customers. I was just being my usual self, but he saw a person with excellent people management skills. *Why don't you pursue your career in management rather than technology?* he told me.

Well, that was new. This is not the direction I had expected our conversation to take. I was obviously flattered and once again took the opportunity for a change in career profile. If I hadn't thought I was being wronged and taken action to correct it, I would never be able to explore another part of my life, which was management.

Don't accept what's wrong for you. Make some noise. Be shameless. You're the one who has to do all these things for yourself because others aren't going to. And why should they? They have their own journeys to map. If you do not say no at that time, then you are wasting your time. And that is exactly what I want you to avoid through this book.

# Chapter 4

## The Values of My Life

<u>*Or, the reasons for my success*</u>

*"Keep your thoughts positive because your thoughts become your words. Keep your words positive because your words become your behavior. Keep your behavior positive because your behavior becomes your habits. Keep your habits positive because your habits become your values. Keep your values positive because your values become your destiny"*
*– Mahatma Gandhi*

I was scrolling through Twitter a few years ago when I burst out laughing at a post by comedian Stephen Fry. He was in his doctor's office in England and there was a poster of the 'Adarsh Balak' on his wall. It immediately took me back to my childhood. I'm sure that's also why the doctor, most definitely an Indian, had put it up. The Adarsh Balak, for those who didn't grow up in the 1980s and 1990s, is a series of posters illustrating the good behaviour of an ideal child. They were a staple of pre-liberalisation childhood in India. All school students would cut up the charts for moral science class assignments.

I always looked forward to the moral science period in school. It wasn't the most popular class, but I enjoyed it because it taught us the good habits we should all inculcate. Two of my favourite Adarsh Balak habits are 'cleanliness is next to godliness' and 'doing your work on your own'. I have always been fastidious about cleanliness. My surroundings are always tidy, clean, and uncluttered. It helps me organise my thoughts better and gives me a lot of positivity and who doesn't want to be in a clean place?

Along with maintaining a high level of cleanliness, I am also a self-reliant person. I realised at a very early age that nobody could do my job better than myself. That way, I rarely have to rely on anyone.

These two were my foundational values, the ones on which others took root and grew. There are seven values that I live by right now. They make me who I am. These values have served me well and are, I believe, the reason for all the success that has come my way.

## Lesson #1: Proactively Respond To Opportunities

Everybody says that opportunity knocks only once at your doorstep. That's not entirely true because we all know stories of second chances. However, it is true for most people. So, if you do not grab the opportunity at the right time, somebody else will do it. This is something I have followed throughout my life. I've taken what's come my way, without thinking if I'll be able to do the job well. I always said 'yes' and then I figured out how I was going to do it.

One of the best examples was when I worked for Wipro Technologies. I was an individual contributor there, a level-two engineer in charge of Microsoft's global backup operations. I had been doing that for one and a half years, and it was time for a change. I had applied for an H1 American visa and had been internally rejected because I didn't have the right qualifications.

Fortunately, around the same time, I got a call from Countrywide Financial. They were looking for a leader who would build a team in India and then build a relationship with their counterpart in the United States. Once that was in place, the manager would have to start transitioning mundane or low-value tasks from the US to the Indian team. In short, they were looking for a manager who had technical experience as well. While I excelled at the latter, I had no managerial experience. But was that going to stop me? No way! There wasn't a moment when I thought that I couldn't do it. If the company had offered me this job, they would have seen potential in me. So why should I reject it? I backed myself, appeared for the various rounds of interviews, and passed!

That's how my managerial and leadership journey began. I often wonder what would have happened if I were a different person, someone who took so much time thinking over an opportunity that it went to the next person. I'm glad I have been able to recognise opportunities that came my way and make the most of them.

We need to do things right the first time because we may never get a second chance, especially in this highly competitive world. This is an extension of the willingness to grab opportunities. Not doing so the first time it happens only means you are delaying your success. This book aims to ensure that everyone who reads it doesn't waste time and attempts to reach their goals as soon as possible. That is why it is very, very important to get it right the very first time.

## Lesson #2: Challenge The Status Quo

I have always believed that one way to measure your growth is to look at the small progress you make. As long as you are on the move, you're headed in the right direction. To do that, you have to devise a way to figure out how you are better today. I do that by challenging the status quo. I ask myself: if this is how things are done, can I do them differently? Is there a more effective way of doing it? Can I automate this? That leads me to answers and solutions I had never thought of before.

People do not like to challenge the status quo because they don't want to take risks. As a techie, I see that often. People are scared to embrace technology because they fear it. They are afraid it will take over their lives, and maybe make their jobs redundant one day. That's not the correct outlook towards the world. We have to embrace what's out there. That's the only way to grow, to be better today than what you were yesterday. Upskilling is a way to challenge the status quo, so is an effective way of communicating or doing a task. How else will any of us progress?

There is a reason why risks and rewards are tied together. To grab bigger rewards, you have to take calculated risks. When I moved to the United States in 2010, I had no experience managing global customers. I knew nothing about American culture either. But when the opportunity came for me to pick up the role of a leader and move to the United States to manage different engagements and customers, I just said 'yes'. Only when I landed in the US did I start figuring out how the culture works, how to meet customers, the right way to greet people, and what they ate. I figured that out as I went along and made it work for me.

And it's not just the professional space that has seen me making changes. I have moved things in my personal life as well to be where I am today. One of them is working on controlling my emotions. I used to be very reactive and known for losing my anger. When I had just started working, I was a very quiet person. But as I climbed the ladder and got bigger responsibilities, I often lost control over my emotions. Fortunately, I realised soon enough that it was draining a lot of my energy. What I needed to do instead was to channel that energy in productive ways. I became a better listener because of that. So then, whenever I got pissed off, I would pause, take a coffee break, and come back to my desk with the ability to look at different perspectives.

And now, I'm proud that I never panic or lose my temper. Others have observed it too and asked me the secret. I'm sharing it here. Control your expressions, control your emotions, and constructively channel all of that.

## Lesson #3: Commitment And Delivery

There's a dialogue actor Salman Khan made famous: Ek baar jo maine commitment kar di, uske baad toh main apne aap ki bhi nahin sunta; Once I have committed, I don't listen even to myself. It's quite silly if you read it literally, but I think his character means that he always delivers on his commitment regardless of the circumstances. Well, that is me.

I have never gone back on my word. It has helped me build trust with everyone at work and in my family. In an ideal world, everyone would be a trustworthy person. But just because it isn't doesn't mean we don't strive to be that person. Trust is one of those rare gifts of life that keeps giving, which is why it has to be an important part of your life. If people don't trust you, you will ultimately lose. In the workspace, if your client does not trust you, you will lose their business. And if you are losing business, you are losing growth.

Trust brings you more opportunities and responsibilities. When I was working at the financial services company, we received a non-compliance fax from Microsoft. To become compliant, we had to buy its licence worth INR 35 lakh. There was no way my boss was going to pay that much money. He asked me to resolve the matter, and I told him I would. It took me three days of almost nonstop work to figure it out, but I stayed true to my commitment. That was the time when the open-source market was picking up. And there was one such platform called Linux that everyone was talking about. But since I knew nothing about it, I went to the market at Nehru Place in Delhi and bought a book called *Linux Unleashed in 21 Days*. After going through it from cover to cover, I locked myself in the room for three days and was able to successfully migrate our entire infrastructure from the Microsoft platform to Linux. And the company had to, in the end, buy only a INR 4-lakh licence. I had saved the company INR 31 lakh. It took a lot of effort, but there was no way I was going back on my word. That's why I was given a promotion out of turn. Not bad for a promise and three days of work, right?

## Lesson #4: Strive For Customer Satisfaction

If you think about it, there is a customer present in every aspect of our life. Sometimes your kids are your customers, other times it's your parents. In the office, it's your boss, colleagues, and clients. These are the people you strive to keep happy regularly. The best way to do that is to step into their shoes. That's how you understand how they work and what makes them tick. It helps you relate to their problems and bring options to the table that are focused on resolving an issue or meeting their needs.

You have to work hard behind-the-scenes to perfect the art of making customers happy. It also makes you better at your work because you will leave no stone unturned to come up with a solution. By going above and beyond the template to satisfy your customer, you will do a lot of critical thinking, be creative, and think beyond constraints and out of the box. You will learn a lot more about yourself than you realised because you're pushing yourself to be as good as possible.

All this adds to the experience you gain and to your success story. Let me illustrate that with an example.

Initially, my perspective on customer satisfaction was shaped by my experience supporting international customers remotely from India. I followed our rich Indian culture of greeting them warmly, always being polite, never saying no, responding promptly, and assuming this approach would keep them happy. And they were happy. I regularly received thank-you notes from customers with messages like 'You are the man' and 'You made my day'. These responses made me feel I was truly satisfying my customers and meeting their needs. It's because of that that I became one of the top performers in my team and was given the opportunity to go to the US to manage my customers and my team.

I soon realised that there are many aspects to customer satisfaction. I was expecting a good score on the year-end satisfaction survey given the positive feedback I had always received. But the same customers who loved me also gave me a rating of only 3 out of 5. One comment from the survey stood out: I feel there was no value in innovation, transformation, automation, or thought leadership. This feedback made me realise that my customers expected more than day-to-day support; they wanted to see how I was adding value to their business and making their employees and customers happy. With this newfound clarity, I changed my approach. We created a dedicated team focused on continuous improvement, innovation, and value-added opportunities. We developed Key Performance Indicators (KPIs) to measure our progress. And in the next survey, we received a rating of 4.5 from our customers.

## Lesson #5: Enable And Empower Others

I had a boss who was a micromanager. He had control issues and believed that only he could do the task at hand. So he hovered over our desks to make sure we completed the work to his satisfaction. It used to annoy me so much that I had made a mental note that if I were ever fortunate enough to lead a team, I wouldn't be like him. And I haven't. I've paid attention to my behaviour and consciously made sure that I am a different kind of boss.

A boss's main job is to get the best out of his or her team members and help them grow. You do that by trusting them to do the job well. And then you have to let go of their hand so that they can prove themselves out there. If you do not empower people around you and give them the keys to the kingdom, they will never be able to use what they've learnt in real life. The only way they will trust themselves is when you trust them.

Think of empowering your team like teaching your children to ride the bicycle. You get them a cycle, you hold them from behind, you run with them for a while, you will leave the cycle sometimes and then you will grab it before they fall. But once your kids have gone through the basic act of learning to balance, you let them go. They may fall, but they will rise again because you have taught them the skills of survival. And then one fine day you will see them zooming past you on the street, not even holding the bicycle handle, their hands up in the air, and enjoying this newfound confidence.

I didn't always have this kind of support when I was a newbie, so I have always strived to be better. When I worked at Cognizant many years ago, one of my team members was a level-one desktop engineer. I saw a lot of potential in him because he always showed interest in work and was willing to learn new things. He was meant for better things, so I made him the team lead. I had bigger dreams for him, but I wanted to do it in small steps. With certain directions, I encouraged him to make his own decisions. That way, he was able to successfully transition some of our projects. I soon needed a transition manager who would be required to go to the US, learn certain processes, and come back home and teach them to the rest of the team. I put his name forward for the job. Even though he wasn't confident he was the right person, I knew he was. I informed him that he should take the lead and I would support him from the backend.

I hand-held him for a couple of meetings and then to build some transition reports. And soon he was flying on his own. After eight weeks, he came back to India with a successful transition. He was so good that our customers rated him 4.5 on a scale of 5; this was when others in his position got scores of 3.75.

He is now what is commonly called 'a big shot' in another company. And I'm proud that I played a part in him reaching there. Few things are as satisfying as seeing your mentee flourish beyond his or her wildest expectations. We can all do with a little bit of help in life. So why not be that for someone else? I guarantee you and they will be richer for it.

## Lesson #6: Be Open And Honest

I asked a primary school child recently about a proverb she could tell me in the next two seconds and pat came the reply: honesty is the best policy. She didn't even have to think about it. It was easy as the answer to 2 plus 2. We have been taught since childhood that we shouldn't lie and always adopt honesty. That's because it is the lightest way to operate. When you're honest and open in every interaction and conversation, your mind is free, and you have a cookie-cutter response because you have nothing to hide. You don't have to worry about getting the story right each time. I spoke earlier about not overprocessing the mind. By being truthful, that is eliminated.

I came to the United States from a culture that encourages secrecy. Indians are told not to air their dirty laundry in public, and everyone is busy hiding their secrets. But American culture isn't like that. They are open people who don't feel ashamed of making mistakes. I was delighted to live differently now because at the workplace, I only needed to focus on delivery. I took this approach of transparency while dealing with clients as well. There have been times when I knew that my team, despite trying its best, couldn't provide the key deliverables on time to the customer. On such occasions, I have informed the customer a few days before the deadline of our inability to meet it. They have always appreciated my upfront approach and given me a few more days of extension. Through this, I learnt that people always appreciate it when you come from a place of honesty and sincerity. Sure, they are tough conversations—it's not easy to admit that you haven't done a stellar job—but at the end of the day, it was a win-win for both parties.

Another reason why it's best to be honest is that bad news never becomes good just because you share it later. It only worsens over time. If my team and I tried to bury our heads in the sand and did not inform our customers about the delay, in the hope that we would somehow meet the deadline, we would have been in trouble. It would take seconds to lose the client's trust. This is, in fact, true for every relationship in your life. Hiding things and trying to brush them under the carpet will never serve you well. Be honest every time and see how stress-free your life becomes.

## Lesson #7: Take Responsibility For Your Actions

We all tend to deflect blame when things don't go our way. We either blame others for our predicament or we'll blame the situation we're in. This starts when we're in school. When we do not score good marks, we always justify it by saying that the paper was tough. Or we say that questions were out of the syllabus. I remember that on every result day, my father would ask me how much I had scored in each subject. I would tell him and immediately follow that up with the marks of the brightest student in the class. The reason was if the smartest kid could score only 75 marks in Hindi, then my score of 65 wasn't as bad as it looked.

I realised much later that by doing so, I was not taking ownership of the fact that I could have studied and performed better in the exam. Why couldn't I own up to it? Because doing so would require some serious introspection and changes that I would have to strictly implement. It was easier to blame everything other than myself for my marks.

I'm glad I realised that and decided to change my attitude. Now I take full responsibility for everything I do. By not blaming others, I have saved myself a lot of energy that is now channelled into focusing on what I should do differently so that I'll be successful the next time around.

The unnecessary chatter that follows the blame game ends the moment you own up. I would rather expedite my growth path instead of wasting time blaming others. When you take responsibility, you own the correction process and ensure you apply the lessons learnt. This approach allows you to make a comeback and bring any situation under control. Blaming others weakens you and takes away a valuable opportunity to learn and grow.

A few years ago, I was chosen to lead one of the biggest and most critical projects that my company had won. It involved a major utility company in southern California, USA. This project was crucial as they generated power using atomic reactors. Our role was to support their IT infrastructure and Enterprise Resource Planning (ERP) applications – both onshore and offshore. They had important mainframe servers hosting mission-critical and business-critical applications, with employee safety as their utmost priority.

However, the transition of the project wasn't going well. Our team struggled to get information from the current one, who were about to lose their jobs, impacting the quality of work and causing us to miss deadlines. The chief information officer (CIO) was upset and asked his accounts team to hold off on any payments related to our services until we presented a go-to-green plan to bring things back on track.

Good leaders have two main responsibilities: take charge when your team is failing, and give them the stage when things are going well so they can receive praise and appreciation. I took responsibility for our actions on behalf of the entire team instead of blaming the resources and circumstances. I created a special team to develop a go-to-green plan. We reworked our plan with new timelines and renegotiated it with our customer, committing to bringing the project back on track. After two months of dedicated effort, we were able to meet all our commitments with the highest quality within the given timeframe. The CIO was ecstatic. He asked his accounts team to release our invoice payment and rewarded us with additional work, which helped us grow our portfolio and revenue with this customer.

These are the values that have worked for me. They guide me every day, and I can proudly say that I have never wavered from them.

They are so easy to follow because they demand from me things I am happily willing to give: hard work, dedication, and honesty. They are the foolproof way to success, and I'd be delighted if you can imbibe even a few of them in your life.

# Chapter 5

# The Art of Trusting Yourself

## *... and why it pays rich dividends*

*"20 years from now, you will be more disappointed by the things you didn't do than by the ones you did do. So throw off the bowlines. Sail away from the safe harbour. Catch the trade winds in your sail. Explore. Dream. Discover." – **Mark Twain***

One of the many things I've learnt over the years is that we are capable of much more than we give ourselves credit for. When I look back at the difficulties I've faced or the challenges I've taken, I'm amazed at how far I have come and all the adversaries I have overcome. It shows me that I have always been made of sterner stuff. If I weren't, there is no way I'd have reached where I am from where I started.

I have dared to believe I would be fine, no matter how bumpy the road. That belief meant I could make professional decisions without worrying too much about the consequences and expanded the possibilities that became available to me.

But I wasn't always like this. That is because no one, including me, is born with immunity to self-doubt or fear of failure. But what we are born with is the ability to learn how to step through our fears to pursue paths that inspire us and change those that don't.

My journey is proof that when you trust yourself—when you doubt yourself less and back yourself more—incredible things can happen.

## Lesson #1: Whatever The Endeavour, Give It A Few Tries

Swiss tennis player Stan Wawrinka has a tattoo of a quote by Samuel Beckett. It goes: "Ever tried. Ever failed. No matter. Try again. Fail again. Fail better."

It's a wonderful quote that everyone should—no, not tattoo—put up somewhere in their room and read every day. It's so inspiring because it asks us to keep trying and keep learning from each try. The lesson from each try will be different, and you may ultimately fail at your endeavour. But you will have failed better than the first attempt.

Giving up anything after one attempt would be a disservice to yourself. What if Thomas Edison had given up the first time his bulb failed to light up? What if J.K. Rowling didn't approach a new publisher each time her Harry Potter manuscript was rejected? You have to keep trying until you know you've given your best. I'd say that three tries are good enough. Attempting something thrice means you have evaluated what went wrong at least twice before going for one last hoorah. And if, after that, it doesn't work out, then it most likely isn't going to happen. Of course, there are exceptions—like the two people I mentioned above—but for most people, three attempts are reasonable. After that, you should look at changing your direction because there is something bigger planned for you.

As I have mentioned in earlier chapters, I gave my childhood dream of becoming an Indian Air Force pilot three shots. The first time

I was rejected, I told myself that I had come so close to being selected. Maybe with a few tweaks, I could make the cut. Hence, I changed my approach and focused on the skills I could acquire to pass the next time. I did that, but it still didn't work. So when I was rejected the third time, I had a hard talk with myself. Was this the right goal for me? If it is, why isn't my performance getting better? Maybe it's time to recalibrate. This introspection gave me a lot of clarity on why it was time to give up. I had given the dream everything I could at that time and I had come up short. It was time to dream some new dreams and pursue those instead.

At that time, it becomes extremely important for you not to brood over the failures. One way I have done that is to think of the entire experience as an institute I had joined. And everything that I have spent learning is the tuition fees I paid to obtain that knowledge. We all pay tuition to schools and colleges to gain knowledge, degrees, and certificates. So why not consider failure as another accolade added to your knowledge base for which you paid a fee? You learnt about failure at the University of Life and now it's time to move on, to graduate.

This approach helped me make peace with the failures and rejections and freed up my mind to pursue other avenues for career advancement.

## Lesson #2: Ask Yourself, 'Why Am I Passionate About This?'

I hear a lot of young people talk about 'passion'. It's the reason they choose a particular profession because they are passionate about it. But are they? We may think that our goals are driven by passion, but scratch the surface and a lot of times it's because of the environment we grow up in. My father and brother were both employed with the Indian Air Force. We stayed in the quarters provided by the armed forces. So, everyone I knew ever since I was a child was related to the armed forces in some way. In my limited worldview, the IAF was probably the only employer in the world. And once I said out loud that I would like to work for them too, even when I was older and could have explored the outside world, I carried that dream along.

Only later did I realise that my childhood 'passion' was nothing but a kinder version of Stockholm Syndrome. I didn't give myself a chance to explore my strengths or find my real passion. I was a dedicated and disciplined student, two qualities that the IAF takes a lot of pride in, and rightfully so. That was also one of the reasons I thought I was the right fit to become a fighter pilot. What I didn't realise then was that those qualities are applicable in almost all professions.

If there were somebody, a mentor or a guide, in my life who would have helped me realise my strengths or asked me some tough questions, it wouldn't have taken me 20–25 years to finally discover my passion.

I realised at a much later age that I love technology. I also love to serve the community and mentor people. Helping somebody achieve their goal makes me happier than achieving my own goals. I now know that I was not meant to be a king, but I would have been a great kingmaker.

So ask yourself some tough questions. Why do you want to be something? Are there reasons you haven't explored yet? Doing that will set you on the right path for you.

## Lesson #3: Leave Your Options Outside The Door

In 2015, I was working at a manufacturing company in the US. Like all tech companies, we also had an enterprise software agreement for three or four years to purchase and use their software. My chief information officer (CIO) had already struck a deal, and I was invited to a meeting with them only so that I could be introduced to the vendor team. When I came to know the cost of the software, I felt we were being overcharged for it. I joined the conversation and said that the amount needed to be negotiated. The discussion went on for some time, and I emerged victorious. I had managed to get my company an almost 100% discount on the negotiated numbers plus an unlimited licence with payment for a 5-year maintenance agreement.

It was a proud moment for me, and my CIO remembered it fondly too because he brought it up at a town hall sometime later. A town hall meeting is a gathering of all the employees in a company at once. He spoke about my negotiation skills and said that if anyone wanted a lesson, they could include me in one of the meetings. And then he said something I still remember: 'Rakesh will sit at the table without his wallet.'

I love this story because it shows how determined I am when I want something. A negotiation implies that both parties will come to a mutually agreed conclusion. Both will give a little and settle on an agreement. But I never concede in a negotiation meeting. You concede a little monetary ground when you have your wallet with you. But when you come empty-handed, you have nothing to give, and the other party has no option but to agree to your offer.

That is why it's good not to have options sometimes. Because when you have one, you know you have a choice and won't fight back with all your might. The knowledge that you always have a backup will ensure you don't bring your A-game to the table.

It's how, I assume, those on a diet will behave. It's better for them not to have chocolates at home than to have a few in a fridge and then decide to exercise control. When the option of eating chocolate whenever you want is gone, you have no choice but to eat a healthier snack instead.

So, when you encounter failure in your professional life and have to recalibrate, I suggest you take all options off the table. That way, you will focus all your energy on your only choice, and then your chances of success increase.

## Lesson #4: Success Is Not Always Vertical

I have spoken earlier about a book called *The Peter Principle*. The author, Laurence J. Peter, writes: 'In a hierarchy, every employee tends to rise to his level of incompetence.' He means that if you perform well in your job, you will likely be promoted to the next level of your organisation's hierarchy. You will continue to go up the ladder until you reach the point where you can no longer perform well. In this scenario, the next step is to move sideways so that you can create room for yourself to grow.

The perfect example of the application of the Peter Principle in my life is when I was rejected at Wipro Technologies for a US visa because I didn't have an engineering degree like the rest of my colleagues. I had risen by sheer hard work. I had taught myself everything the job required based on the Microsoft certifications I had received. I had reached the upper limit of my competency for that job, and there was nowhere else to go. I was given a lifeline when I decided to quit and was instead suggested that I should look at a career in management. It was time to move sideways because the ladder to climb up had been moved. I took up my boss's suggestion and enrolled for an MBA at Symbiosis

University in Pune and started the journey that has led me to where I am.

Had I been fixated on reaching the US through the role I had at that time, I would have failed. I needed to move sideways to create the upward journey. So be open to the possibility that your idea of success may not be the right one. Once you do that, you'll be more open to exploring other avenues that can take you to your goal faster.

Every time you encounter a roadblock, know that you have hit a ceiling. Now it's time to get creative, do some introspection, and figure out a way to make room for yourself. You could move sideways, but at least you're moving. And when you're moving, you're progressing, you're growing.

## Lesson #5: Think Of A Bigger Problem And Your Current One Will Shrink

As a child, I was a bit of a fussy eater. So, whenever my mother cooked something I didn't particularly like, I'd protest and ask for something else. And my mother's answer was always the same: think of the kid on the street who probably went to sleep hungry. That would shut me up, and I'd quietly eat dinner until the next time it happened, and the cycle continued until I became older and my palate expanded.

I didn't know it then, but my mother was teaching me an invaluable lesson on managing problems. By asking me to focus on the bigger issue, she was eliminating the threat I perceived from the smaller one in front of me. I had no business complaining about the food served to me when just down the road lived a family on the footpath who struggled to make ends meet. Ever since

I understood the meaning of what she unknowingly taught me, I have always tried to focus on the bigger problem to make my current one manageable.

When I was rejected for the third time by the armed forces, I did not go back home that night. I was so devastated and incredibly sad that I spent the night on a bench outside a temple. But the next day, when the sun's rays woke me up, I was a different person. I realised that my failure was not my parents' fault and they should not be punished for it. They were worried sick about me and they didn't deserve it. Another reason I was eager to go home was that I now had a bigger problem to solve: what to do for the rest of my life. That was such a big question I needed to answer that the event of my failure seemed small.

I, frankly, had bigger things to worry about and that's where I had to focus my energies, not on what had already happened. I call this deliberate diversion of your mind **brain-train**. You have to take control of your thoughts and train your mind to focus on the most important thing at that time.

Think of the time your stomach was hurting badly. Even after taking the necessary medicine, your condition isn't better and now it's too late to meet a doctor. What do you do in that case? Try to divert your mind so you don't focus on your stomach. You watch a movie or play some games on your phone. That doesn't stop the pain, but it does take your mind off it for some time until you can do something about it. This same principle of brain-train applies in every aspect of your life. When you look at the bigger picture, you realise how small your current worry is. That gives you the perspective you desperately need at that time and clears your mind to think of solutions for the bigger problem instead.

## Lesson #6: Don't Waste Your Time Turning Your Weaknesses Into Strengths

I often hear people talking about converting their weaknesses into strengths, of how someone hot-headed and reckless rebranded these characteristics as 'passionate' and 'innovative'. That's a whole lot of humbug, and when you scratch the surface, you realise there's nothing substantial inside.

I find this endeavour a waste of time. I haven't seen more than a handful of people turn their weaknesses into strengths. But the rest of us can only bring our weaknesses to a manageable level. That too takes a lot of effort, and the progress is very incremental. That's why I'd rather you focus on your strengths because that has a higher chance of giving you success.

The Pareto Principle, also known as the 80/20 rule, is a theory which says that 80 per cent of the output from a given situation is determined by 20 per cent of the input. So, wouldn't you rather focus on the 20 per cent (your strengths) if they will give you an 80 per cent success rate? I know which option I would choose. If you choose to go the non-Pareto way and focus on your weaknesses, you'll put 80 per cent of your energy into managing them, only to get an output of 20 per cent.

My biggest weakness used to be procrastination. I'd leave things until the last moment and then hurry to finish them. I could have given it a positive twist and said that procrastination has helped give my brain time to mull over a task and create space for greater creativity and innovative ideas. But that's just glossing over the truth that I was undisciplined with my time. Thankfully, I grew out of that habit organically and didn't have to waste time turning it into a fruitful endeavour.

On the flip side, I did take forward one of my greatest strengths, my personality. I don't consider myself an individual; I think of myself as an entity. It gives me the ability to step out of taking an individualistic approach and allows me to focus on representing multiple facets that make up an entity. I have always been a good storyteller and have worked on enhancing this by speaking well, talking about engaging topics, showing a genuine interest in what someone has to say, and generally doing my best to make a great first impression. This has developed my personality even further and helped me immensely in my people-facing career.

All of us are a lot more capable than we think and can contribute more than we know. It's all about letting go of self-doubt and trusting yourself as much as possible. If you can do that,

What changes would you make?

What new goals would you take on?

What chances would you take?

# Chapter 6

## Keep Your Friends Close

_The inner circle of friends and mentors who have been the guiding forces of my life_

_"The people closest to me determine my level of success or failure. The better they are, the better I am. And if I want to go to the highest level, I can do it only with the help of other people. We have to take each other higher." – John C. Maxwell_

We are all suckers for great friendship stories. The comforting presence of a friend who understands you and wants the best for you is a joy that everyone deserves. Growing up, the adventures of Jai and Veeru in _Sholay_ (a famous Bollywood movie) were a delight to watch, and I have always worked to build that kind of camaraderie with my friends.

But do you know what's better than having a wonderful friend? A friend who is also your mentor. That's what Bill Gates had in the form of Warren Buffett. Bill had credited the scale of his success to the help he received from Warren, his friend and mentor. 'Warren isn't just a great friend. He is also an amazing mentor. I have been learning from him since the day we met in 1991,' wrote Bill in a blog in 2015. Meta's Mark Zuckerberg also received mentoring from Apple co-founder Steve Jobs when Facebook was experiencing a rough patch in the company's early days. Steve invited Mark to India, where he was on a spiritual journey to reflect on and reconnect with his vision for the company. They continued to have a mentor-mentee relationship and a friendship until Steve passed away in 2011. At that time, Mark expressed his admiration for Steve on Facebook and wrote, 'Thank you for being a mentor and a friend. Thanks for showing that what you build can change the world.'

We need to be surrounded by good people. Such people have the power to change the trajectories of our lives. They guide us, correct us, invest in us, and show us the right path. But mentors don't just fall into your life. You have to seek them at every stage of your career, whether you are just starting, midway through, or even thinking about retirement. Good, successful people who wish the best for you are a rare breed. So when you find them, learn as much as you can from them. Observe how they conduct themselves, what they are good at, how they spend their free time, the way they speak, and many more such things. And then apply that in your life. In an earlier chapter, I spoke about how success leaves a strong footprint and the easiest way to be successful is to follow the footprints of those who have excelled.

I had three such mentors and friends who made a significant contribution to my career as well as my personality development. I have known them through various phases of my life and I have always looked up to them as someone I want to be. They have all taught me some important lessons that I am now passing on to you. These lessons have served me well and I will forever continue to use them.

## S.N. Ravichandran

Ravi was my first manager at NIIT. He was about seven to eight years older than me when I joined his team as a graphic designer with no experience. My first interaction with him wasn't friendly or positive. I believed he was playing favourites and not thinking about everyone on the team. But my opinion changed when we went for an office outing, and I saw a completely different side to his personality. He thought like me, spoke like me, and we had similar interests. My preconceived notions about him started to change, and we soon became close. Just shows us why the first impression isn't always the best one, and we should keep our hearts and minds open about people. Here are a few things he taught me that I remember and follow to this day.

## Lesson #1: Accept criticism from the right person

The world is not a fair place, and everyone doesn't always have your best interest at heart. When you do encounter such people, it's best to ignore their opinion of you. They don't know you well, and their statements could dent your confidence. However, there are many like Ravi in the world as well. People like him notice your potential and want you to excel.

Ravi never shied away from criticising me, especially in front of others. He knew that public criticism would not cow me down, that it would be the making of me. He knew I wouldn't go into my shell if I was criticised but would come back stronger to prove him wrong.

It's tough to listen to all the ways you did a job wrong, that too in front of your peers and colleagues. Whenever I would present him with my work, he would find the faults first. My initial reaction would be to accuse him of being too picky. But he continued with his suggestions on how I could make the art better.

I realised much later that all Ravi was doing was pushing me out of my comfort zone. That was the turning point for me. I took his comments positively and started to feel very blessed that a senior manager like him was interested in me and my future. Criticism from the right person can set you on a faster path to success. The key is to identify who wants you to flourish and follow their advice.

At NIIT, I was a high performer in my team. I was among the few graphic designers who were also visualisers. One part of my job was to interact with instructional designers and work on the storyboarding exercise with them. I didn't have the patience for that, and I believed I was more efficient on my own. So, I would create my design elements instead of engaging with the rest of the team. I was also a little lazy because I didn't want to waste time explaining the concept to someone else; I could do it faster. So, I would make the initial frames of the storyboard on my own. Visualisers worked with their team leads, who reviewed the frames and provided feedback, after which the instructional designers would review them again.

Ravi would attend these review meetings whenever my team was presenting because he was looking out for me. I don't think he did that with other teams. He wanted me to stay grounded and not get carried away by the praise I would end up receiving. He was strict with his feedback because he knew that would bolster me to do better and prove him wrong. This was Ravi's roundabout way of making sure I didn't get too big for my boots and to remember that it was my work that would always matter, not my opinion of myself.

There were two reasons for his presence at these meetings. Ravi wanted me to learn, and he encouraged me to come out of my comfort zone and remain grounded.

## Lesson #2: Invest in yourself

Ravi taught me that everyone should work towards their personal growth and well-being. And he did it by never telling me this. At NIIT, I earned INR 3,200 a month. I didn't make enough to splurge on the finer things of life. At that time, Ravi earned INR 27,000, which was more than what the president of India earned, which, I believe, was INR 18,000 a month. He was always sharply dressed, and he carried himself with a quiet confidence that I wanted for myself, too.

I saw Ravi dressed in Allen Solly and Van Heusen clothes, which was considered the best office wear at that time. I wore clothes from either Janpath or Sarojini Nagar, Delhi's roadside fashion streets. Ravi introduced me to South Ex, a posh area of Delhi, and a famous clothing store in upmarket South Extension called Snowwhite. He planted a dream in me of becoming a smart, fashion-conscious person like him. Ever since then, I've been particular about the way I present myself.

Ravi was also an excellent photographer and came back from his first trip to the US with a Nikon DSLR camera. He pursued his hobby in his spare time and I'm glad to have witnessed his absolute love for it. Through his life, Ravi taught me the importance of living life as a king-size. He showed me that we work not just for money but also to feed our hobbies and passions.

## Lesson #3: Don't Get Emotional About Work

We are all proud of the work we do. It sustains our souls and gives us an identity that we carry for the rest of our lives. And that is even more true when we are in the initial stages of our careers. I was the same too. I was excited about any work that was assigned to me and dove into it with gusto. And I got carried away on quite a few occasions.

As a graphic designer and visualiser at NIIT, I used to get very emotional when I was assigned a project. I always wanted to give my best, and because of that, I would come up with seven to eight options. That's a lot of work for something that didn't always merit it. That's when Ravi would enter the picture and tell me to give myself a break. I wasn't helping myself by working so hard, nor was I helping our customers. In fact, by presenting so many options, I was only confusing them. Instead, I should pick the three best designs and know beforehand which one I liked the most. That way, I could steer the customer towards what I liked instead of flooding them with options.

That was a very smart move on Ravi's part. He channelled my energy into creating three good pieces of art instead of eight. That saved me a lot of time and taught me to distance myself a bit from work. It gave me some much-needed perspective on conserving energy and not over-delivering when it wasn't necessary.

## Lesson #4: You Can Work Well With Someone Even If You Don't Get Along

NIIT encouraged a culture of working with everyone in the team. So, while small teams were created to handle different projects, they would be mixed up, and members rotated so that everyone got a chance to work with everyone else. That way, I worked with multiple team leaders. On one of those occasions, I was working with a leader who was known to be a tyrant. She was quite strict and expected everyone in her team to always perform well. She even made a few people cry with her harsh criticism.

I had heard horror stories about her, so naturally, I was a bit apprehensive. But she went on to become one of my best friends at work. I never had any issues working with her because I knew when to draw the line with her. She was pretty demanding and was known to stand behind our desks and monitor the work we were doing. But I didn't work well with micromanagement. I knew I had to stand up to her and display an even stronger personality. So, every time she stood behind me to check my progress, I would lock my screen and walk away. Soon enough, she got the message that I wasn't going to accept her controlling behaviour. That's when the negotiations began. We both learnt how to not piss off the other person and, in the process, created a very strong, high-performing team.

It was only later that I realised that Ravi knew all along that she and I would be a great combination. That's why, when the three months were up, and I was to move to another team, he told us that we were always going to be in one team. And I was never moved from her team. This is what good bosses do. They know the strengths of their juniors and get the best out of them. And I learnt that you can gel well with someone you don't particularly like.

Ravi and I aren't in touch anymore. He slowly faded away from my life, but I will always wish him well and am eternally grateful for everything he taught me.

## Bhagwant Singh Sarhadi

The second person who has played a huge part in how my career was shaped is Bhagwant Singh Sarhadi. I worked with him at the privately held finance company in Connaught Place, Delhi. He led the application development team, so he was my boss's peer. Bhagwant is also the one who interviewed me, so I knew him from day one.

He and I initially bonded over chai and sutta (cigarettes) during work breaks. I used to be a smoker then, but thankfully, I have managed to kick the habit. We also had an Indian Air Force connection because he retired as an officer from a Short Service Commission. He was placed in the same department as my father and stayed where I grew up–the Air Force station in Rajokri, Delhi–so we always had plenty of stories to share.

I didn't realise when all those chats at the local tea stall led to a genuine friendship that endures to this day. Bhagwant has been with me through all the ups and downs of my career and life.

## Lesson #1: Always Err On The Side Of Practicality

Bhagwant was, and still is, an extremely practical person. As you may have realised from the preceding chapters, I am an emotional person, and sentiments have ruled my head and heart when I have made decisions regarding my career. But Bhagwant taught me that being practical brings a lot of rewards in its wake. It allows us to adapt quickly, make informed decisions, and move forward despite the challenges we encounter. Bhagwant's practical side meant that he always had mental clarity and workable solutions for all problems.

He was a great planner and used his time efficiently. At that time, he used to stay in Faridabad on the outskirts of Delhi and travelled to Connaught Place by train. He read the Economic Times on the way to stay up to date on one of his great hobbies: investing in shares. Bhagwant used that one-hour-forty-minute journey to come up with an investment strategy, and by the end of it, he would know which shares to buy and sell. He forgot about all that the moment he reached the office. He gave his all to work till it was time to leave at 4 p.m. and also when the stock market would close for the day. He would quickly make changes to his stock portfolio and use the rest of the journey home to read books.

Bhagwant is the reason I began picking up motivational books to read as well. I bought the first impactful book, *Who Moved My Cheese*, from a second-hand book stall on the footpath near Connaught Place. These books started to bring about a change in my approach and perception of life. And I have Bhagwant to thank for it.

Being practical also means mixing romanticism with a dose of sensibility. I have always been a man of high principles who takes great pride in having idealistic thoughts. However, relying on idealism without thinking about the real world can be foolish. Bhagwant asked me one day if I believed in God. I grew up with the presence of God in my home, and I have taken that with me wherever I go. I told him I worshipped Saraswati, the Goddess of knowledge. Bhagwant's immediate response was, 'Tu bhooka marega' (You'll die hungry). I was puzzled; why would I struggle in life? Especially when I believed in the power of knowledge.

Bhagwant had the answer. At our office was a small temple because the company's managing director strongly believed in astrology, and he was God-fearing. We even had a pandit who would conduct pujas regularly. Once, Bhagwant took me to meet the pandit, who introduced me to another Goddess. Sharada was a mix of Lakshmi, the Goddess of wealth, and Saraswati. Bhagwant gave me an all-knowing smile, and I knew what he wanted me to learn. That knowledge without the means to make a good living from it is useless in today's world. We should learn with the intention of monetising it. Since that day, I have been a follower of Goddess Sharada.

My friend not only changed my strong belief system, but he also took my head out of the clouds and forced me into real life.

## Lesson #2: Take Care Of Your Friends

I love reading *Winnie the Pooh* books. They have powerful life lessons for kids and adults. One of my favourites is: A friend is one of the best things you can have and one of the best things you can be.

When I quit the investment firm when they accused me of getting kickbacks, I lost touch with many people. I considered these colleagues my friends, but our relationship faded when I left the company. But Bhagwant was different. He would call me every day and remind me that this was just a tough phase that would end soon. He helped me search for new job opportunities, a kind act I will never forget. He made it a point to meet me whenever he could. The Okhla train station was closer to my house, and it was one of the stops on his way home. So he would get off, and we would meet at a nearby chai-wala (tea stall). He gave me a patient ear at that time, and our conversations always motivated me to do better. I cherish those talks so much and fondly look back on them as one of the building blocks of my life. Of course, he would never let me pay for the chai and samosas. Bhagwant took care of me when I was at my most vulnerable. He never let me forget who I was and instilled in me a confidence that I possess to this day. Because of him, I know that no matter what life throws at me, I will bounce back. What an amazing feeling that is!

A couple of months after I quit, I got an offer from Wipro Technologies. Bhagwant was the first person I informed. If he came to Hyderabad for work, he insisted that we meet at the airport or his hotel. We have stayed in touch even now when I don't live in India anymore.

This constant connection with Bhagwant ensured I never lost hope. When I joined the call centre as a trainer, he would patiently listen to all my stories and say, 'Hey, you know what? This is great. I didn't even know there were so many rules for pronunciation.' I always felt that I was making progress every day just because my friend was there. I had other people I could confide in, but I didn't want to bother or worry my parents and siblings with my stories of struggle. Bhagwant filled that gap in my life by ensuring that while I was fighting my next fight, he was around.

Bhagwant is now the head of corporate insurance at a big company, and I'm sure he continues to be a great mentor and friend to his colleagues there as well.

## Sivaram Tadepalli

When I left NIIT and Ravi, I immediately connected with Bhagwant. The moment I relocated to the US, Sivaram came into my life. So, there was no period where I was without a mentor or a guide.

Sivaram was my client partner; he was a peer to my boss, but he handled a separate vertical within my company. Usually, there are tussles between various teams at IT companies because while one focuses more on customer relationships, the other concentrates on revenue. But there was great synergy between Sivaram's and my teams. On the first day we met, he told me that he was about to retire but decided he needed to rejoin the workforce to help pay her college fees. His transparency was refreshing, and I'm glad that he trusted me, a stranger, with details about his personal life. That set the tone for our relationship at work and outside.

## Lesson #1: Appreciate Others When They Do A Good Job

Sivaram is an alumnus of the Indian Institute of Technology (IIT) at Kanpur and the Indian Institute of Management (IIM) at Ahmedabad. Later, both his brothers followed into the IITs. I held him and his family in high regard because of their incredible academic accomplishments. Sivaram has told me on quite a few occasions that I remind him of his father, who loved everything to do with technology. Tadepalli Senior worked at a time when technology wasn't a part of people's everyday lives. However, he embraced tech after retirement and taught himself a lot of things with the help of Google. I am astounded that he saw his father in me. Coming from an IITian, it was high praise indeed, and it remains one of the best compliments I've ever received in my life.

Sivaram never lost an opportunity to boost my confidence. He did that by simply acknowledging my work and appreciating it. He has told me several times that I always come up with innovative solutions to problems, something he isn't very good at and how he could have never thought of the solution that I came up with. He noticed that I always treated the company like it was my own. It had a marked effect on my work ethic and my performance.

We were also each other's sounding boards. Sivaram would always tell me, 'I will not be able to tell you what will work, but I can certainly tell you what will not work.' So, when I used to come up with solutions to problems, I'd first approach him for his opinion. That has saved me a lot of time and effort.

## Lesson #2: Show The Ropes To A Newbie

When I moved to the US, I was naturally nervous. I had never stayed outside India and was unsure of whether I would find my feet here. I was apprehensive about my ability to assimilate into an alien culture. And I was glad that Sivaram was around to guide me. I used to be the person who rarely made eye contact in a conversation. Instead, my eyes and mind would wander about, thinking about the next thing to say. But Sivaram taught me about the importance of eye contact. After hearing about it enough times, I finally did what he wanted me to: raise my face and look into the eyes of the customer.

That is just one of the many things he taught me. I learnt so much about this country and its culture, and also about topics like mathematics, science, and language from Sivaram. He has been by my side as I grew from an unsure person to a self-assured one. He and I made our two teams work at a time when no one else was able to bring about peace in departments with conflicting interests. At that time, I got the highest award from my company that anybody would have received in the delivery team. Sivaram always ensured that I was recognised, and I'll always be grateful for that.

## Lesson #3: Never Forget The Importance Of Being Diplomatic

All workplaces can become volatile at times, with situations that require deft handling so they don't escalate into a full-blown wrestling match. On one occasion, a critical team member had put in his papers in the midst of working on an important project. I had to immediately fill his position. Sivaram asked me if I knew of a worthy replacement. I did, but he had just been assigned to another project in Europe. Poaching colleagues from other teams is frowned upon, but he was the person I needed for my project. How could I get him without ruffling any feathers? Sivaram was the one who got the job done.

He intervened on my behalf and set the wheels in motion. He spoke to one guy, who spoke to his leader, who spoke to my leader, and between them, it was decided three days later that the team member was released from that project. He had been immediately instructed to leave for the US and join my project. Sivaram helped me handle that situation diplomatically while keeping me in the background so that my relationships with colleagues wouldn't be spoilt.

In this situation, Sivaram and I played like a team. We had our own diplomatic way of problem-solving, using the principle of divide and conquer by breaking the problem into smaller sub-problems.

## Lesson #4: Be Fearless

It's easy to say that we should forget our fears and just do what the heart desires. But to do it every day so that it benefits your life in every way requires some practice. The only way to lose fear is to be smart and take the plunge. That's what Sivaram taught me.

All large IT companies work on an onshore and offshore model. About 10 per cent of the team is on-site, with the rest of the delivery being done from offshore places like Bangalore, Hyderabad, or any other Indian city. The distance and lack of Facetime invariably lead to misunderstandings and souring of relationships between these two teams. I was part of the on-site team in the US, and my offshore team had accused me of deliberately not making a project work. This reached the senior leadership, and a meeting was to be held where I was assigned the responsibility to deliver a get-well plan to the customer.

But how could I create a plan that would be executed by the offshore team over whom I had no control? I was under tremendous pressure from my leadership team at that time. No one was willing to take ownership of the problem, and they were looking for a scapegoat.

I didn't know what to do and shared my anguish with Sivaram. He thought about it for a couple of days, and his suggestion was to speak with the customer about it and transparently tell them about our constraints and challenges that would potentially impact a successful outcome. What was Sivaram suggesting?! It was ludicrous. Why would I share the company's internal problems with the customer? I felt that this was not ethical. But Sivaram told me that our job was to make the customer successful. That was our goal and our duty. It was time to show our customers the difficulties we had been facing for them. Sivaram gave me mentorship and courage at the crucial juncture. And what an incredible piece of advice that turned out to be!

I called up the chief information officer (CIO) of the customer company and sought a face-to-face meeting. I spoke to her about the issue we were facing and if she had any solutions. The CIO was glad I had brought up the matter to her and told me that she would handle it at the big meeting planned with all the teams involved with the project.

On D-day, when I started the presentation, the CIO interrupted me and said, 'Hey, we always hear from you. Why don't we hear from Rajesh, the offshore boss, instead?' Rajesh was the senior-most member of the offshore team. I have, of course, changed his name here. Rajesh had no idea what solutions to present because he wasn't clued in at all. All I can say is that that meeting was not good for Rajesh. The CIO wasn't kind to him and his lack of preparation and understanding of the issue. I share this story here because I wanted you, the reader, to know how Sivaram and I worked in the best interest of our customers. That's what our company—and hence us—was legally bound to do.

Shivam's advice saved us a lot of time and ensured that my company's relationship with the customer did not deteriorate. We created a good impression of our company in front of the customer.

Over time, I realised that it takes just one attempt to kill fear. And that move he and I made was that attempt. After that, I have never been afraid of approaching a customer and being transparent about challenges and how we could team tag to ensure a successful outcome. Now, I am comfortable having any kind of conversation with anybody at any level in any organisation if I believe that it serves my company well. And that is what Sivaram taught me.

These are the three most significant people in my twenty-eight-year professional journey. Their mentorship did not just remain a part of my career development, but it also became part of a lot of my personality development.

Ravi, Bhagwant, and Sivaram have seen me change from an introverted person into a fearless leader. Many others have played a part in getting me to where I am today, but they stood on the shoulders of giants like Ravi, Bhagwant, and Sivaram. They made me the man I am today.

# Chapter 7

# It's Time to Act Smart

## How a bit of jugaad goes a long way

*"Do the best you can until you know better. Then when you know better, do better." – Maya Angelou*

All of us want to succeed. We'll never meet anyone who says they'd like to fail. But, as we all know, wanting something doesn't mean we'll get it. Failures and rejections are an inevitable part of all our lives. The key is to have more successes than disappointments. So, what can we do to improve that strike rate?

What's worked for me is making smart—and sometimes calculating—choices. People these days call it Chanakya Niti. That may be true, but I would call that being clever. As I write this book, I can think of three occasions when I had to be a little crafty to get closer to my goals. Making those decisions has led me to where I am today.

## Lesson #1: Make Things Happen For Yourself

The first one took place at Wipro Technologies. I was so happy to have got a job there and thought I was now set for life. I planned to stay there until I retired because, in my mind, I had made it and there was nowhere else to go. Life, as always, had other plans.

I want to share an extremely funny incident that took place on my first day there. As I mentioned in a previous chapter, I applied for a job at a call centre called SpectraMind after I saw a hoarding of it in Delhi, which was a call for applicants for technical roles. I ignored the advertisement at first and kept riding my scooter as I had already been shortlisted for a technical support role with Convergys. It was an outsourced support company for Cisco in those days. But after continuing for 3 kilometres, something called me from within and took a U-turn at the next traffic signal and applied to SpectraMind as I was jobless and desperately looking for any engagement. I was initially ready to accept any job offer at any compensation. But when my interview went well, I asked for INR 20,000 a month. I was surprised when they agreed. INR 2,40,000 a year, more money than I had ever seen in my life. At that time, I realised I would be working for Wipro and not SpectraMind because the tech company had acquired the call centre.

The day I joined, after the onboarding formalities, we were given food coupons. For lunch that day, I got into the elevator to go to the cafeteria on the top floor. A man with grey hair got out of the lift. I turned to my friend and asked why this company was hiring old men. Turns out, that was Azim Premji, the founder of Wipro. One more facepalm moment. Since then, I've always done my homework on the companies I have joined and the women and men who run them.

I was hired as a Technical Consultant at Wipro. I was happy with that title because, in the outside world, a Technical Consultant means a more serious and valuable IT role. It also came with higher compensation. But there were a few on the team who wanted to be called Technical Leads. I did not want our designations to be changed to that and some of us protested. The dispute didn't die down organically, and the head of human resources had to travel from the Bangalore office to Delhi to settle it. Luckily, I was on the day shift when she arrived so I could meet her. I told her that we had discussed the matter internally among ourselves, and everyone agreed that Technical Consultant was the designation they were all right with. She was relieved and signed our offer letters and left the same afternoon.

Yes, I lied to her that day because there was no consensus. But I did so for my—and the greater—good. A Technical Consultant title carried more weight and would let future employers know that we had a certain set of skills, which would only be more beneficial for us. I didn't regret it then, and I don't now either. Everyone else who was not on board later also got bigger opportunities only because of the "Technical Consultant" designation.

That conversation with HR was enlightening in another way too. She told me about the concept of the bench that Wipro Technologies had. It maintained a pool of resources that would be ready to be deployed to any new projects. I had been assigned to work on an American bank called Washington Mutual, which was seized by federal regulators and rapidly acquired by J.P. Morgan Chase in 2008. We were to provide technical support for their US employees. The role was more on the lines of a call centre and a help desk. I wasn't really interested in doing that and was looking for a way to get out of it, and the bench provided the perfect opportunity to do so. I told my friend about the plan and he was on board too. At Wipro, Technical Consultants would be trained for 15 to 20 days and then the customer would pick about fifteen people that they thought would be ideal for their project. My grand plan involved my friend and me not being one of the chosen fifteen. In that case, we would be placed on the bench, and other clients would be free to choose us. The best part of this job was that even if you weren't chosen, you wouldn't be fired. So it was a win-win from my perspective.

So my friend and I actively worked to be rejected and became a part of the bench. That worked out great because the next client was Microsoft, which was looking for people for its project in Hyderabad. My friend and I both got selected, and off we went to Hyderabad. This is one more place where my Microsoft certifications held me in good stead.

This is how I applied some good old Chanakya Niti and got myself rejected. This smart move took me a long way – to Hyderabad – to the then biggest software company in the world.

## Lesson #2: Take Up Jobs That Advance Your Career And Pay You More

I quit Wipro about a year and a half later when I was unable to move to Microsoft. I had joined Countrywide Financial, which was at that time the number one privately held mortgage company in the US. Later, it was acquired by Bank of America during the subprime mortgage crisis in 2008. I had a managerial post there. How I got the job at Countrywide is also an interesting story.

A headhunter approached me for the job. I didn't know much about it and gave the interview at night because the top guys worked in America. They asked a lot of technical questions that I was able to answer, and I passed Round 1. I knew Round 2 would be tough. So I prepped well. I already had one computer at home. I rented two additional computers and set up a technical lab at home. I practised all the possible scenarios of backup technologies with master and media server and tape libraries because I didn't want to let this opportunity go. That must have done the trick because I was able to clear the second round as well.

Next, they wanted me to fly to Mumbai. Countrywide was willing to send me a flight ticket and pay for my accommodation as well. This was my first brush with how companies outside India operated, and I was suitably impressed. I had travelled by air a couple of times before that, so it wasn't a completely new experience for me, but I was nervous nonetheless. This was also the first time I wasn't spending my own money to travel.

All that worrying amounted to nothing because Countrywide's Executive Vice President, on learning that I worked the night shift for Microsoft, didn't want me to ask for a shift change. He didn't want to trouble me and said they would set up a video conference instead. Reliance had set up Web Worlds across cities, and I had to show up at one of them for the online meeting. If I was nervous about flying earlier, now I was practically sweating. I didn't know if video conferences were expensive and worried about how I would pay for them. This was in the third week of the month, and I was running out of money. I sheepishly asked the receptionist how much I would have to pay. To say I was relieved when she said Countrywide was taking care of it would be an understatement. I immediately went out for a smoke to celebrate that moment of relief.

At Countrywide, I was paid double what I earned at Wipro. I had persuaded a lot of my colleagues here to enjoy the perks of earning double. I had hit the jackpot and I shared it with my friends. I was at Countrywide for more than two years when a job opportunity presented itself. My boss at Wipro called one day to inform me that he was moving to Cognizant and asked if I'd like to join him. I was always ready to move jobs for better experience and pay, and agreed. I appeared for an interview and they offered me the job, with a salary of INR 14 lakh. In just three years, I had moved from earning INR 20,000 a month to over INR 1 lakh a month.

I was just waiting for my last working day at Countrywide and then relocating to Bangalore to join Cognizant. But just a week before I was to leave, I got a call from Computer Associates (CA). They were looking to fill a senior managerial position urgently and thought I'd be a good fit. The CA office was close to Countrywide's so I dropped in for a quick interview and they immediately offered me the job and they were willing to pay me INR 16 lakh a year, INR 2 lakh more than Cognizant. No points for guessing what I did next. I accepted their offer with a huge smile, and one conundrum: how would I tell my ex-boss that I wasn't going to join him after all? I did break the news as gently as I could later and all was well.

There may be some people who read this and consider my choices reckless. But I did what I thought was right for me. Only an unwise person would reject the offer of a higher salary and the opportunity to experience different projects at different companies. All of my friends had moved far ahead even though we had all started together, and I was determined to at least be a promising participant in the race.

There is an anecdote I'd like to share before I move on.

It's about the time I was quitting Wipro to join Countrywide. I emailed my boss after I accepted Countrywide's offer about my resignation. I didn't log it into the system officially because my boss was convincing me to stay back. In all this back and forth, the official two-month notice to Wipro hadn't begun. When my boss realised I wouldn't budge, I made it official. However, the HR department refused to let me go on the date I wanted to because I now need to serve my notice period. I was livid! It wasn't my fault if my boss was not ready to accept that I wanted to quit. I had an email to prove the correct date I put in my papers. I was asked to meet the Regional Director of Wipro Technologies in Hyderabad. Suffice it to say, the conversation did not go well and a few volatile words were exchanged.

We had to be separated, and I left in a huff. Fortunately, Countrywide, being an American company, did not want me to submit a relieving letter from Wipro. The way I exited the company did leave a bad taste in my mouth, but I had no other option.

I put it behind me when I landed in Mumbai to join Countrywide. Things got brighter when I was asked which laptop and BlackBerry model I preferred. I was also asked to submit my passport for an American visa so that I'd be ready in case I needed to travel for work. I had been waiting eagerly to hear these words. I told my friend in Hyderabad to visit the Chilkur Balaji temple. It is more famously known as the Visa Balaji temple because most people visit it and wish for their visa to be granted. Believers undertake eleven circumambulations before visiting the visa office and 108 after the wish is fulfilled as a mark of gratitude. It sounds funny, but it has its believers and I was willing to do everything it would take for the visa gods to grant me my wishes.

And it worked! I visited California soon after on my first-ever work trip abroad. However, I quit soon after because Countrywide became a part of Bank of America and with the change in management, it was time to move on, as I mentioned earlier, to Computer Associates.

## Lesson #3: A Few Tweaks Here And There Will Help You

My time at CA was quite fruitful; we grew our customer base and developed a lot of business in Europe. I even travelled to Munich to set up another data centre. But this stint also ended because of a less-than-stellar boss. He would make all of us managers compete for small prizes. It was quite annoying to have to fight for INR 500 vouchers, especially when you had no interest in doing so. Seven months in, my Wipro boss, who had been trying to recruit me for Cognizant, called again.

I was quite fed up at CA and asked Cognizant to match my salary. They initially refused, saying I hadn't even completed a year at CA. But they soon relented, and I quit CA after nine months and joined Cognizant in Bangalore.

I had a good time working there. All my projects were at the top of the chart, and every new hire wanted to be a part of my team. It was a giddy feeling, and I was revelling in it. But just a year in, I was bored and restless. I was performing exceedingly well, but I wasn't learning anything new. Was it time to move on again? I was contemplating that question when Bank of America (BoA) called me, asking me to join them again, this time as the Vice President. They were offering me INR 25 lakh as an annual salary, which I was happy with. I was ready to go back to Hyderabad. But, of course, life had other—bigger—plans for me.

I had informed my boss at Cognizant about my decision to quit. As we were working out the details, I was speaking to one of my counterparts in the US Cognizant team one day, and he told me that he, too, was looking to move on to another opportunity within the company. And then he gave me a brilliant idea. Why don't I talk to my boss about moving me to his position in the US?

My colleague had been at Cognizant for a long time and he was aiming for a bigger role in the company. We had become good friends during our time there. I told him I didn't think it was right for me to make this suggestion to my boss; it would be more authentic and convincing coming from him.

We practised our lines, and I spoke to my boss the next day. He, of course, didn't know it was a staged conversation. I told my boss that I had decided to accept the offer from Bank of America. At that time, my mind went to my initial Wipro days when I talked my way out of one project and into another. My boss called my counterpart in the US as soon as I left his cabin. My colleague then delivered his lines beautifully; it was an Oscar-worthy performance, even though I didn't have a chance to watch it. He feigned shock, took a couple of moments to calm down, and said he had a plan. He told my manager what we had discussed. My boss was sceptical; he wasn't sure I would accept. After that call, my manager came to me and told me he had an offer for me – he would place me in my counterpart's position in the US. That way, I'd get a different, better opportunity, and I wouldn't have to move back to Hyderabad.

Bingo!

Our plan had worked. I was finally going to have the chance to push the accelerator on my career. And this time I was going to make sure my visa would come through. In a previous chapter, I spoke about how Wipro Technologies refused to process my work visa to the US because I was an arts graduate. I mentioned that to my boss and asked how he would ensure that I wouldn't face obstacles this time as well. He had an answer ready. He would apply for the visa in the L1 category. The L1 visa was comparatively easier than H1B and has better chances for permanent residency (Green Card).

I wanted my boss to bring up the L1 category, instead of me having to say it. I still wasn't sure if he would follow through with it. But 15 minutes later, I got an email that my L1 visa had been initiated. It was a happy day, and I was extremely glad that the plan had succeeded.

I chased the company's travel desk to get a visa appointment as soon as possible, and after 15 days, I was in Chennai for it. The passport and ticket to another life had finally been placed in my hand.

You know that saying about good news coming in threes? Well, my streak was continuing. As my visa process was going on, a Cognizant colleague, Harshe Gautam, who had lived in the US for a few years, came back home to India. I was appointed as his buddy to teach him about how offshore operations work. While passing on everything I was doing in Bangalore, I told him about my plan to move to the US. After that, I couldn't stop all the knowledge he wanted to share with me. He told me about how Americans operated, how much compensation I should expect from Cognizant, the approximate monthly expenses my family and I would incur, and a lot more. And then he gave me the best piece of advice, something I needed at that time.

At Cognizant, my designation was manager. He told me that managers have to wait for a year before applying for a Green Card. But if I went there as a senior manager, I'd have to wait for only six months. That was extremely helpful information. Cognizant had two appraisal cycles: one in April and the other one in August or September. Our conversation took place in March, and I was due for a promotion in a month. I didn't make it through the promotion list in April. I knew that if not April, August would most definitely see me as a senior manager. The moment that happened, I started pestering my manager. I wanted to know when I would move to the US.

He told me in October that I could leave in a couple of months. And in December 2010, I landed in the US with my family. The first thing I did when I checked into the hotel was turn on my laptop and set up a reminder for June 2011 to apply for my Green Card. Lo and behold, in just six and a half months after I applied, I got a Green Card in the EB-1 category, which is available for foreign nationals who either have extraordinary abilities or are a multinational executive or manager.

This is how I ensured that I matched up to my peers in achievement and salary. My initial experiences at the workplace were marred with conflict and impulsive decisions. In retrospect, I'm glad that I didn't suffer any career setbacks. But I did lag considerably when I compared myself to my school or college mates. That is why I was determined to not let such opportunities pass me by.

I don't think what I did was devious. It wasn't illegal either, not by a long shot. I just used the information I was given smartly and set in motion plans that would ultimately work in my favour. I did that by keeping my eyes and ears open for anything that would be useful to my career growth.

All my moves—from Wipro to Countrywide to CA to Cognizant—were done because I was looking for exciting work and believed that the salary should reflect my commitment and excellence at work. I was ready to move cities—from Delhi to Hyderabad to Mumbai to Hyderabad to Bangalore—and did not stay in my comfort zone. These constant jumps added to my skill set and increased my salary regularly. And with a bit of Chanakya Niti, I made a few things work for myself.

Eight years of my work life, from 1996 to 2004, were slow. I was frustrated with the frequent bouts of joblessness. And even though I was changing jobs, I wasn't moving up the career path. But the next four years were when I experienced multi-fold growth, and I finally made it to my destination, America. The land of opportunity opened avenues for me that I had never thought possible. I gained global exposure in every aspect of life – personal, professional, cultural, social. And it led me to two of my most successful side hustles: real estate and technical consultancy.

## Lesson #4: Develop Your Interests And Follow Through With Them

There is just something about confidence. It does beget success. When you're on a hot streak, confidence gives you the strength to go after what you want with even more gusto. It can make you feel like you are hovering two feet above the ground. You feel you can get anything you want.

When I moved to the US, my confidence was sky-high. The world was my oyster, and I wanted to explore as much as I could. I stayed with Cognizant for a few months after shifting countries, and the itch to work at another place needed to be scratched. This time, I wanted to work at Tata Consultancy Services (TCS). I had always aspired to work there because it is India's largest IT company by a huge margin. But I knew they wouldn't entertain my CV because they want engineering candidates who have performed exceedingly well at the class 10 and 12 stages. And I was a student with a science, commerce, and arts background; it would have been too colourful for the straight-laced company that TCS is. But I was now in the US. That made a huge difference. And when I got a call from a headhunter about an opening at TCS I could apply for, I was ready to give it a shot.

I had seventeen rounds of interviews before they decided to hire me. Seventeen! When the offer letter came, I wished I had asked for more because they gave me everything I had asked for. I had dreamt of working for TCS for several years and now it had finally come true. However, it turned out to be a less-than-stellar experience. My team wasn't the best. There was a lot of red tape and bureaucracy at all levels, and people were not making decisions on time.

But I did my job diligently when I was there. Regardless of my opinion on the company, I had been hired for specific tasks and I wanted to complete them without bailing out on TCS. One of my responsibilities was to fix their release management process and event management process. Our customer was already unhappy with the delays, but I didn't have a magic wand to fix the problem. I asked for an extension of two months, which was granted after some negotiations. At that time, I put everything in order, and the CIO and CFO were so pleased that they asked TCS's accounting team to send our invoices. That was the day I quit. I was there for only nine months because TCS and I weren't a good fit.

I had already received an offer from SC Johnson, a company that manufactures household cleaning supplies and other consumer chemicals. I had a great time there and I stayed there for five years. That was a personal best for me at that time. At SC Johnson, I played the role of a customer for the first time. At every other job before that, I or my company was service providers.

My stint there was uneventful but successful. After five years, my CIO at SC Johnson quit the company and joined SpartanNash. It's a Fortune 500 company that works in food distribution and grocery store retail. He wanted me to join his team at SpartanNash but because he had a non-poaching agreement with SC Johnson, he couldn't hire me directly. That's when I started a consultancy, which I run to this day. I started by providing my services to SpartanNash itself and other customers before I was officially hired. The first thing that struck me a few days into my independent work was that there is so much money in tech consultancy if you do it well.

Three years into the consultancy, , I was offered the job of Chief Technical Officer (CTO), which I accepted. So, that is how I started my consulting firm, BeyondCX, where CX stands for customer experience. I currently provide mentorship to several start-ups in India.

I'm so happy that my first foray into running an independent business has been a success. I love technology and how it changes our lives every day. It's this love that has sustained my business. My interest in finding solutions and making work easier for other businesses is why my entrepreneurship journey has been a great one.

The confidence boost I got from my thriving consultancy led me into the world of real estate.

I studied economics in college and realised one very important thing: the fluctuations of the stock market weren't for me. It works on pure speculation and is governed by a few companies. I have never invested a penny in the stock market. What I have parked my money in is gold and real estate. I like that they are physical things I can touch and feel. An unfortunate incident also had a part to play in my interest in real estate. When I got my first house in the US, I had to deal with a lot of water damage when a frozen pipe burst at a time when I was in India. The situation was so dire that 75% of the house had to be rebuilt. I worked closely with the contractor at that time and picked up quite a bit of construction knowledge.

I have always loved how homes are designed, but my actual interest in real estate started in 2023 when I came across a video on YouTube about building two rental properties in a year. I was very impressed with that video. They talked about a BRRR technique, where you buy, reconstruct or rebuild, rent, and refinance a property. I have also bought homes to rent them. It sounded like a fun project that would also yield good profits. Even though the video only spoke about working on two properties in a year, I laughingly set myself a target for 10. It seemed like a pipe dream, but I still can't believe that I made that dream come true. I started in April 2023, and just 13 months later, in May 2024, I was able to add a significant few to my portfolio. Even if I say so myself, what an incredible achievement!

I'm glad I have been able to understand the minutiae of market dynamics and the rate of interest in real estate. Working on the first few houses was a learning curve, but I soon learnt how to take advantage of the market.

There have been huge takeaways from everything I have done. I changed all my jobs when there was a recession. Of course, I didn't plan it that way; it's how the opportunities worked out. I was advised by several people around me to stick to my job because the recession had caused volatility in the market. But I still stuck with my gut and took those opportunities. Similarly, every time I invested in a property, every economic and financial expert would say that the US was going to go through a recession and that doing so would be a wrong move on my part. The moral of this story is that people may say whatever they want, and data may say something, but your assessment and your judgement are all that counts. People consider too many external factors while making a decision. Why do that? If I had paid attention to the naysayers, I wouldn't have made a profit.

Access anything based on your situation, not on market conditions. A lot of it depends on your risk appetite. Only you know how much risk you can afford to take and whether you have the mental fortitude for it. Others don't, and hence can only guide you. Move forward with the knowledge that every decision of yours won't always land. You will fail too. Can you afford to fail? Do you have a safe space to land if things go south?

That will go a long way in helping you make the right decision.

I also believe in the 80-20 rule. Eighty per cent of people will always tell you not to do something because they are part of that group. If you want to be part of the 20 per cent—the people who are decisive and tell others to be that way too—you have to do things your way.

When you follow your interests, you build a lot of confidence in your ability to get things done. Be smart about your choices, back yourself, and see how far you can go.

# Chapter 8

# The Joys of Learning

## _Why being a lifelong student will always pay dividends_

_"Never stop learning, because life never stops teaching."_
_– Unknown_

A friend of mine has a five-year-old who is the naughtiest boy I have ever met. To get him to sit in one place is an impossibility and something even his parents are struggling to enforce. He's a competitive little boy and loves to play games. So along with the usual outdoor sports, they've enrolled him in a chess class. The one-hour class is the only time—other than mealtimes—he sits for that long. He does so because he loves learning new sports, and chess is his latest obsession. He loves trying to outsmart his teacher and their banter in class.

What struck me most about this is how partaking in something engaging can have a profound effect on us. And we're even willing to change because of the enjoyment we get from it. That's the power of learning.

I've always found learning to be my best friend. Immersing myself in a new skill or course makes me extremely happy. And on a practical level, none of us can afford not to learn. It's something we cannot get around or away from. If you want growth, you will have to keep learning. As everything around us changes, we need new skills to keep up with the new world. Our older skills won't have much value sooner or later. So, learning is a very important part of growth.

I am a lifelong learner. It's a quality I'm proud of. I'm always looking for ways to better myself. Whether it's my personal or professional life, if I come across an opportunity to be better tomorrow than I am today, I will go for it.

## Lesson #1: Learning (or not) has brought you to where you are

Since you've read this book so far, you'll know that my professional life's trajectory has been an uncommon one. I am a student of multiple disciplines. My willingness to pick up various certifications and experiences meant that even though I wasn't qualified for the tech world by way of a college education, that's where I ended up. You are unlikely to find anyone without a BE or B.Tech or BCA or MCA degree in this field. I had neither. But here I am today, the CTO of a Fortune 500 company in the US.

The Microsoft Certified Systems Engineer Certification programme opened up a world of opportunities for me. I'm so happy that my friend enrolled me for it and I followed through with it. I have often wondered what would have happened to me if I had been the obstinate sort, the kind of person who would have resented this interference from a friend. Certainly nowhere close to where I am right now.

If I didn't have the hunger for more, I'd have dismissed my friend's suggestion. There are a lot of people who are happy where they are in life, and there is nothing wrong with that. But if you aren't happy, if you want to bring about change, learning something new is the best and easiest way to achieve it. Instagram is full of stories of people who picked up a new habit or hobby and found themselves in a new life a few years later. That was me, and it could be you.

## Lesson #2: Your Weaknesses Can Be Your Biggest Strengths

When I first came to the US in 2010, I must admit that I suffered from an inferiority complex. I had worked at large tech companies like Wipro and Cognizant. I had been doing well at work, well enough to be transferred to another country. But the fact that I didn't have a tech degree like my colleagues always rankled me. I had graduated in arts with a major in economics and political science. That was not helpful in any way when it came to my work. I had also been unfairly judged by my former bosses who had tried to hamper my career prospects for not having the right degree.

However, when I came to the US and introduced myself as a graduate in economics and political science, people were impressed. These subjects are given a lot of respect here, and excelling in them gives you major brownie points. Suddenly, the things I valued least became a huge confidence booster for me. I learnt that no matter how much we tell people not to judge a book by its cover, it happens. Unless somebody opens the book and reads it, they won't realise its actual value.

I was determined to learn new skills because they would make my book cover—my CV—much more attractive. That way, people will at least attempt to know what I bring to the table. That is how I began taking courses from various colleges. I have now picked up courses that have interested me at Cornell University, the Massachusetts

Institute of Technology, Berkeley, and Stanford. They have helped me immensely at work and in my everyday life.

## Lesson #3: A Lot Of Times, You Already Know The Lesson

In 2017, I came across a course on Servant Leadership at Cornell University. Yes, you read that right. At that time, I too was surprised by this name. It sounded intriguing, so I signed up. Servant Leadership is a philosophy built on the belief that the most effective leaders strive to serve others, rather than accrue power or take control. It follows no hierarchy, and the leader works alongside their team, rolling up their sleeves and getting their hands dirty.

As the days went by, I realised that Mahatma Gandhi, Nelson Mandela, and Mother Teresa all followed this style of leadership without knowing about it. And I was like them too – with a much, much smaller impact on the world.

I have always been close to my team. Because they do their job well, I have the privilege of being their boss. They ensure that I am employed. A lot of bosses hesitate to interact with their team in a real way. They are happy to delegate and send out emails for tasks that have to be accomplished. That's not me. I like to get into the everyday nitty-gritty of work. How my team makes customers happy is of great interest to me. The course also gave me a lot of insight into how the US marketplace functions.

This course was a good example of knowing something without realising it. It showed me that what I was doing with my team, consciously or unconsciously, was the right thing for all of us. While it didn't teach me anything new, I was now more aware of what I had been doing. The knowledge that's out there is sometimes in you too.

You just don't know it. All of us are repeating history in some form or another. While that may not make us pioneers, we are pretty good at following in their footsteps.

## Lesson #4: Application In The Real World Is What Makes All Learning Exciting

In earlier chapters, I mentioned a book called *The Peter Principle*. One of the most striking things about the book is how it talks about growth. When you grow professionally, you are closer to the ceiling. That leaves you with less and less room to grow. So what do you do in that case? Stagnate? Of course not. The only option is to push the ceiling.

That is why I kept learning at various universities. And I applied those lessons at work. At Berkeley University, I did a course on Technology Leadership which gave me a holistic view of a world beyond technology. I was now able to put myself into the shoes of my coworkers, my counterparts, or leaders across businesses. How technology can save the company in the long term is something I learnt more of in the course. It taught me how to tell a story to my company's board when I go there seeking funds.

Let me give you an example. At the Fortune 500 company I work at, the biggest challenge for any technology leader is technical debt. Every asset that you buy has a lifespan. For instance, a server or a switch for networking generally has a depreciation period of seven years. It can run for a few more years, but by that time, the technology becomes obsolete. In technical terms, it's called end-of-life and end-of-support. Once your asset reaches that level, you become very vulnerable to ransomware attacks. A hacker can easily get into your network, causing a huge reputational loss for an organisation. So one of my jobs is to always stay ahead of the curve and ensure that there is always funding in place to refresh these ageing technologies.

So, earlier, when I used to go to the board asking for money, I was always asked about how the money spent would help the company to build its topline. And my answer was that there was no return on investment for this because this was part of the company's tech foundation. Not investing in updating technology leaves you at the risk of being compromised. It was a tough sell. I rarely received the full amount I asked for because I struggled to explain to the big bosses how critical the upgrade was. The board always thought that it was better to spend funds on purchasing new trucks since we are in the supply chain business or fixing damaged roofs at our distribution centres.

The Berkeley course gave me the skills to translate what I was unable to communicate earlier into a story that the board of directors could understand. It brought value to my arguments. I could now help them better understand how these upgrades would enable our business to tap into the latest technologies and bring more robotics and automation into our system. That would help us deliver faster, reducing operational costs and impacting both the top and bottom lines. When I changed the story, it became an easy sell.

I also solved a similar issue because of my learnings in the course. One of the biggest challenges a retail company like mine faces is replenishing its stock on the shelves. It's a very human-intensive activity. You constantly need people moving around at your store, going through the aisles, and looking into every stock-keeping unit to check how many products are still on the rack and how many should be replenished. No company wants a customer to enter a store, not find the product on the shelf, and leave.

The company was looking into automating the entire process, which they could only do because they had already fixed the tech foundation. They would never have been able to bring in any new robotic technology because it wouldn't have worked with the aged network technology that we had. So, the board immediately saw the value of what I was saying and permitted me to upgrade the network that could bring in more robots into the workspace. That cut down the processing time by a huge margin.

I was able to tie my story with these problem statements. The course helped me do that. I brought the knowledge from the course to the boardroom and shared it with my business leaders. Before Berkeley, I did a course at MIT on Digital Transformation in Supply Chain. It pertained to the work my company does, so there were many learnings I could apply in my job. The importance of robotics came from my course at MIT and then the storytelling part and how to convert it into a business statement was something that I learnt from Berkeley.

## Lesson #5: Learning Will Impact Your Personal Life Too

How we live and what we will leave behind for our children is a topic that interests me. Some time ago, I came across an article about how close we are to consuming our carbon credit. A carbon credit is a way of compensating for emissions of carbon dioxide or other greenhouse gases. It is a reduction, avoidance, or removal of emissions to compensate for emissions released elsewhere. That article alarmed me so much that I struggled to sleep that night. I thought about the poisonous atmosphere my children would breathe in when they grew older and how even surviving would be difficult for them.

It got me interested in the Sustainability programme that Stanford University offers. I thought I knew the harm humans have caused on

Earth, but I didn't know how bad it was until I started this course. The state of the world right now is unimaginable, and I shudder to think of what future generations will inherit. That article and the Stanford programme have compelled me to make some serious changes in my lifestyle.

Since then, I have tried my best to drive my electric car rather than the petrol one. I have stopped using a wood-based firepit because I don't want to contribute to the carbon footprint. I've logged into all my bank accounts and selected the 'no paper statement' option. I have installed solar panels on my roof. These are small changes I have brought about in my daily life so far, and I will hopefully be making many more soon.

We don't do all our learning from schools and colleges, do we? The University of Life has a lot to teach us as well. I have reached a stage in my profession where I don't think I can create more room for growth. When I look back at all that I have experienced and achieved, I believe I have done far more than I ever thought I could. And when you reach the stage I am at right now, you start thinking about giving back.

In 2023, I started a non-profit after my mother passed away. It has two goals: to provide education to the underprivileged in India and to develop a culture of entrepreneurship among the youth of the country.

With the new trust, I'm trying to provide these kids with some real-life experience. The Indian education system is great for teaching concepts without giving students any exposure to the world outside the walls of the classroom. Students will take at least a year to know how things function out there and are then ready for whatever challenges their job throws at them. That is a waste of precious time at an age when graduates should be disrupting the system.

With help from the foundation, these kids can be productive the day after they get their degree and don't need any on-the-job training. We give them all the skills that are currently needed by the industry along with their curriculum. It makes it easy for them to get a job.

I take them through project management, communication, and time management skills. I also invest in start-ups to give them a seeding fund to develop a prototype that can one day change their world. I have also done their personality profiling, which measures the dimensions of an individual's personality. This has given me a unique insight into each of the students, so I can give them all the tools and techniques they require way earlier than their peers so that they come out of my foundation as true professionals that companies will pick and deploy. I'm sure these kids will be very effective hires for their employers. My ultimate hope is that they generate employment through setting up small-scale industries as entrepreneurs.

## Lesson #6: Learn From People Around You

There is something you can learn from every place if you want to and keep your eyes and ears open. I spoke about starting my real estate career in the previous chapter. It all started with the video I saw on YouTube by Thach Nguyen. He is an internet personality and a real estate investor and developer. He makes such wonderful, informative videos that someone like me with no experience or prior interest in real estate was convinced that he had some strong arguments to make. And now, thanks to this stranger, I have an extensive portfolio of my own. Thach Nguyen was the starting point, after which YouTube's algorithm took over. Videos related to real estate kept popping up on my feed, and I kept watching them and making notes. He and I are both perfect examples of how even people we have never met can inspire us to explore new possibilities.

The beauty of learning is you never know where it can happen. Many years ago, I came across the now bestseller, *Think and Grow Rich*. I remember thinking what a wonderfully strange title it had. If all we had to do was think about becoming wealthy and we would, the world would be a completely different place right now. But it grabbed my attention enough for me to pick it up. After reading the book, I can also attest that the human mind can achieve anything it thinks of. I—a person with a mishmash of an arts, commerce, and science education—took that belief to heart and worked on building an aspiring portfolio. A couple of years ago, I would have never thought that this would happen to me. But I made it happen for myself and I'm so proud of that.

There are learning opportunities all over the place. We only have to keep ourselves open to them. You can't do that if you're judging a book by its cover. Try to understand what a person is saying, educate yourself about it, and then if it makes sense to you, make that investment. We need to have a very open mind. That is where I would always say the same thing that we discussed: never judge a book by its cover because you never know what that book may contain. So, do not apply your judgement. Whenever there is a learning opportunity, just make an investment; you never know what new avenues it might open up for you.

So when I say we can also learn from people, I don't just mean what they say. You can look at how they operate and emulate the things they have done. I have never met Thach Nguyen, nor Napoleon Hill, the author of *Think and Grow Rich*. But they have had such a profound impact on my life even without knowing it that all I can say is 'thank you'.

Let me give you another example. A few years ago, I was invited to a manufacturers' conference in the city of Detroit. All companies that manufactured products for the supply chain and retail were present there. I was invited and my curiosity was piqued because I thought I might learn something there. When I was younger, I would attend such conferences for the free stay and food, and the stress-free good time that was guaranteed. But I'm older and, hopefully, wiser now. So whether the agenda of the conference is of interest or not, I respectfully sit and listen to every speaker there. I never underestimate what they have to say.

One day, I was speaking with a person whose company manufactures seats for all the big automakers. He was certainly in the right place because Detroit is the automobile capital of the US. I realised then that car companies don't manufacture everything in-house. They source a lot of it from other companies and then assemble it in their factories.

This gentleman's father had started the company, and he took it to another level after giving it his professional MBA touch. Name a car brand, and they buy their car seats from this man's company. I was hooked. While speaking with him, I realised how much automation is used to keep costs low in this competitive market. He was doing such a great job that he manufactured every car seat in the US and could meet the price of Chinese manufacturers. That was just incredible!

He invited me to accompany him to the factory of a robotics company, which had also participated in the conference. It was a Japanese company called Fanuc that made all sorts of base robots. They make the huge metal arms car companies use to perform tasks like welding and painting. They make the main motor and the base of the robot in Japan and then bring it to the US where the software is loaded at their manufacturing plant. It was such an impressive tour. The factory was full of robots ranging from 2 kilos to 4,500 kilos lifting capability. Although what they were doing didn't have anything to do with my work, I couldn't stop myself from being amazed at the work robots can do. I got a lot of lessons on automation from that conference, something I wouldn't have known at all if I hadn't accepted the conference invite. I could have easily skipped it, but because I wanted to know what sort of technology different companies use, I travelled to Detroit.

Attending such conferences and the online classes I have signed up for has one huge advantage: networking opportunities. Most classes these days—online or offline—comprise 40 to 50 students. All of them are in various stages of their careers; some are top management like me, others have a few years of experience under their belt, and some are even in their early 20s. This has led me to interact with a diverse group of individuals. I hear their unique stories and I find that very productive. I bring an outside view to the organisation. Thanks to this additional knowledge I have gained from people outside my world and the opportunity to network with leaders across the industries have been extremely beneficial.

One of the new habits I've formed is to invest at least 10% to 15% of my annual earnings into my development. It could be formal or informal training, and online or classroom courses. Whenever something piques my interest, I do a bit of research and zero in on a programme that best suits my needs. It's held me in good stead so far, and I hope to continue soaking in as much as possible.

We have no option but to continue reinventing ourselves because we are all living in a changing world. The requirements and needs of companies are changing. What was essential yesterday becomes obsolete tomorrow. So we have to look at where the world is going and evaluate where we are in the scheme of things. If there is a gap in your skillset that you can fill, you owe it to yourself to do so.

Just as we build our homes, buy cars, and set aside money for our children's education, we should invest in ourselves. That's the only way to stay relevant in this ever-changing world.

# Chapter 9

# Signing Off

## *A few final thoughts*

As I wrote this last chapter of the book, I found myself feeling sentimental at times. I'm not one to indulge in nostalgia, so I'm surprised by my thoughts. I suppose we get so busy in our everyday lives and trying to reach our goals that we don't always pause to look back at how far we've come. And I have come a long way.

At 20, I thought I was standing at the beginning of a straight road that would lead me straight to the ladder attached to a fighter jet cockpit. I would have never thought then that I'd end up in the US working in the tech field. It shows me we are all naive when we're young and don't know how unpredictable life can get. That straight road I had envisioned never materialised, and I ended up on a winding one that took my career and me forwards and backwards for a long time.

I hope what you've read in the preceding pages has been helpful. As I said at the beginning of this book, I wish someone had told me all this so that I'd have had an uneventful professional journey. But I guess if it hadn't been all that I went through, this book would not have existed.

I'd like to share a few final things before I end this book. They aren't so much career lessons as they are life lessons. Think them over and you'll realise why I think they are important.

## Don't Postpone Your Personal Life For Your Career

Yes, this book is about attaining professional success faster. But we don't live just to work, do we? We all have full lives outside work, of which our family and friends are a huge part. We have to take them with us as we move along in life.

I just met a guy once who drove this point home rather well. He was going door to door to find out if people were interested in installing solar panels in their homes. I was, and we got talking. He looked pretty young, and I assumed he was in college and doing this as a side gig. Turns out he was young and married with a ten-month-old daughter. And he had taken up this job recently so that he would be able to give a comfortable life to his family.

This is a pretty common thing in the US. People marry and start a family when they think it's right for them, and not when they think they have reached a financial milestone. In India, however, young people work and work until they have 'settled down' and then start to think about their personal lives. They waste a lot of precious years when they could have had a supportive family, someone who was with them every one of those years of struggle.

I got married in 2001, but we had our first child in 2007. Looking back, I wish we hadn't waited so long to start our family. My wife and I were thinking too much about our career, growth, stability, and bank balance. We wanted all of that in place before we made the big change.

Don't postpone your life plan based on your career. There is no guarantee that things will fall into place once your career is sorted.

Trust me, you will figure out things as you go. Waiting for milestones to occur can become a long waiting game. If it's something you want, go for it now – when the time is right instead of waiting for the right time. Similarly, if you want to travel, do it. You'll find a way. Don't wait for your retirement to see the world. Do it when you're young and your knees work well.

We have only one life. Try to make it as good as possible so you can enjoy the fruits of your labour. The time spent with family and friends is priceless. A few more rupees in the bank isn't going to be a substitute for the people who bring us joy.

There is a saying in Hindi, 'Poot kapoot toh kyun dhan saache, poot sapoot toh kyun dhan saache.' It means that if your kids are useless, there is no point in saving money for them. And if you have good children, the same applies because they don't need your money to take care of themselves and succeed. What is required is balance. Enjoy the moment you're in. Enjoy your time with your friends and family. Life is not mathematics; you don't have to look at it as a balance sheet.

We're not machines or robots; we are human. So we should act like humans and nurture our relationships. As long as your personal life doesn't overwhelm your professional life, you'll be fine.

## If You Don't Take Control, Destiny Takes Over

Some people believe in destiny, thinking that no matter what they do in the end, fate will decide the course of their lives. And then some believe in hard work and in its power to trump destiny. I, however, believe in both. Fate and hard work play their roles in our lives. And we decide which one is more important at every stage in our lives.

Think of it like a river. It starts from a glacier and flows through vast expanses of land to finally meet the ocean. That is its destiny. But when it is flowing, a river has a lot of uses. One of the main ones is the generation of power. Water in its natural, free-flowing form does not generate any electricity. But with kinetic and potential energy, turbines, and hydropower plants, we can produce electricity. Similarly, building a dam can channel that water into canals and make barren land fertile.

It's a great example of how changing the river's destination can change its fate. If its course hadn't been changed, the water would have ended up where it was destined to be—the ocean—by default. But because action was taken, that water was used in different ways.

Except for a few initial bumps, I have always been in control of my career. I have made decisions to the best of my knowledge and stuck by them. And I'd like to continue that.

My biggest concern at this time is that I'm running out of time. When you're running out of money, you will look back and wonder where you wasted it all. But I don't have that worry. I had a very clear vision at the very beginning of my life that I wanted to give back to this society. And I'm racing against time to do that. I do not want to leave this planet with a debt. I'm looking for avenues to help those who need a hand to climb up the ladder.

A lot of people tell me that children are our legacy. While that is true, it may not always go the way you are planning. I want my son to be a doctor because I want him to have the power to change people's lives for the better. But he's still quite young and may have different plans. So if I can support somebody else in becoming a doctor, then I'm happy.

I have also let destiny play its part in my life. If I had not worried so much about my career, if I had let things happen the way they were, maybe I would have had kids earlier. And by this time, they would have already graduated. Freedom from their responsibility would have let me retire early, and I would have been fully ready to provide my services to society.

## Do Not Compare Yourself To Anyone

I'm not the first person to say this. Because it's so obvious. Why would we compare ourselves to another person? Other people have had different lives. Their experiences and mental outlook aren't the same as yours. Your capabilities and drawbacks are dissimilar as well. There is no good enough reason to explain why comparison matters. Both you and Sachin Tendulkar have two eyes, hands, feet, a nose and a pair of ears. Does that mean you can play cricket as well as him? Hardly. He is blessed with skills that few of us have. So when you wouldn't compare yourself to Sachin, why do the same with your classmates or friends?

I did that once when I was in class 8, and it ended up in a fiasco. Thankfully, I was old enough to understand how stupid I had been and vowed to never do that again. I have stuck to my promise and never tried to compare myself with anyone ever again.

I was an above-average student in school. I was not the class topper of my class and never aimed to be one. I aimed to always be in the top five. And as long as I was in that, I didn't care about my marks. But one time, I was in class 8 and the class teacher returned our unit test answer sheets. I had scored very low in one of the subjects. I hadn't expected that, so my best friend Raju Dey and I started comparing our answer sheets. He had scored well, so I wanted to know where I had gone wrong.

For one of the questions, he and I had both written the same answer. But while the teacher had given him full marks for that answer, I had received a zero. That was surprising. Raju suggested that I should take both our sheets to the teacher and show her the mistake she had made. That was my big mistake. I'm not sure if the teacher was in a bad mood, but she looked at our sheets, cross-checked the answers, and struck off Raju's and gave him a zero. I was dumbfounded for a second, and Raju's reaction was worse when he found out.

I approached the teacher, hoping she would give me full marks for the answer, but instead, she did the complete opposite. I felt terrible. I had hurt my friend in the process of trying to do something good for myself.

That was the first and the last time I compared myself with anyone. I have made a conscious effort not to repeat that mistake of many years ago and have been successful.

Another argument for why there is no need for comparison is that I have never met anyone similar to me. Apart from the three mentors I mentioned in an earlier chapter, I haven't encountered another person who had much in common with me or had a path similar to mine. Everyone's goals and paths are different. They may have also struggled like I did, and they may have also failed. But their story and the path that they selected won't be like mine. Say, for instance, both you and your colleague are marketing managers. You may be assigned similar tasks at work, so on paper you are contemporaries. But your colleague has a child, and you and your partner have decided to remain child-free. So the drive he will bring to work will probably not match yours because you both have different life responsibilities.

For most of my 28-year career, I have had a technical role. As has Microsoft's Satya Nadella. But how we both arrived at our technical jobs couldn't be more dissimilar. He was an engineer who came to the US for an MSc degree. He was hired by Microsoft soon after and he rose through the ranks to become its CEO. Now look at me. I studied science until class 12. Then I moved to the commerce stream in my first year of college. And then I moved again and graduated with an arts degree. I have never heard of anyone who has done this.

So while comparing is out of the question, what you can do is emulate a few things from people's lives that you admire and wish to imbibe. What you can't do is try to copy other people's lives. No two people can have the same fingerprint. So, every life is unique. Your path can cross at times, but your challenges and goals will always be special.

## You Need Just One Attempt To Face Your Fears

A few years ago, I went on a long road trip across the US. I drove from Maryland on the east coast of the country to California. It was just me, the car, and the road. A road trip was one of the things on my bucket list, and I wanted to strike it off. But my wife wasn't interested in the 'madness' I was about to partake in.

So off I went. Road journeys in the US are a unique experience. There are long stretches in remote areas where you won't find another car on the road. Sometimes service stations were located after 200 miles. I was alone for 36 hours with no one to talk to. But not once did I feel lonely. It takes a lot of courage to do a task as mundane as driving on cruise control alone, but I was glad I did it. I would drive till about 2 a.m. and then check into a hotel. Driving at night took me back to an incident from my childhood that drove the fear of darkness away from my life forever.

I used to be petrified of darkness as a child. It was even more pronounced when my mother would send me to fetch something from a nearby grocery store. The problem was that our street wasn't well-lit. Every time she sent me on an errand, I would wait under the last functioning streetlight and wait for a passer-by on foot or a bicycle to walk past me. I would follow them to the next working streetlight.

My fear came to a head in 1988. The Euros were on, and West Germany was the host. My father loved football and watched as many tournaments as he could. At that time, I was preparing for my class 10 final exams when Euro matches would be telecast in India at 11 p.m. This was a time of satellite television and antennae on building terraces that would catch the signal. Sometimes a gust of wind would move the antennae, and someone would have to physically climb the pole they were mounted on and set them right until the telecast became clear. This was rarely a straightforward attempt because every time you moved it, a shout would come from below, whether to continue because nothing was visible or stop because the telecast could now be seen.

That day I was sent upstairs to fix it. Now our antenna was perched on a pole. We had a 7-8 feet staircase that led to the pole. It was dark up there, and I was alone. I didn't want to be there so badly, but I didn't have a choice. The gods weren't on my side either because it took 15 minutes of manoeuvring for the visuals to finally show up on the screen. Only I know how long those 15 minutes lasted. I was also angry at myself for being 15 years old and afraid of the dark. So on the way back, I forced myself to walk instead of running downstairs as quickly as I could.

That simple act took away years of being scared. I had finally lost my fear of darkness. After that day, I would go anywhere you would ask me to at any time of the night. And it was all thanks to Euro 1988. I learnt that you need only one attempt to kill any fear you have.

## And finally, don't forget to have fun!

What's life without fun? Boring.

Yes, there is a lot to accomplish in life. Goals to meet, bucket lists to cross off, relationships to nurture, and money to be made. But those are always going to be around. There will never be a day when you realise that you've met all your goals. New ones would have replaced older ones before you even knew it. Money, as we all know, is rarely enough. We will keep working for more. To break this relentless journey, we all need to remember to have fun regularly. Go on trips with your family and friends, do things you enjoy, and enjoy the company of your loved ones. All these activities will give you a much-needed break from the rigmarole of everyday life.

When I was working at NIIT in Delhi just after college, my friends and I would grab every opportunity to leave the city. We never wasted our time in Delhi on long weekends and would visit nearby destinations in Uttar Pradesh, Rajasthan, or Haryana. One long weekend, my manager mentioned we should go out of town, and we packed our bags. What was supposed to be a three – to four-day vacation turned into a fortnight.

We were young and travelled on a whim. Our plan would always be to meet at the Inter-State Bus Terminus (ISBT) and decide where to go. We would meet at a cinema hall next to ISBT, have some chhole bhature (an Indian snack or street food), and decide where to go based on the buses leaving shortly. On this occasion, we saw a tourist from abroad standing in the queue for a ticket. She didn't know how India worked and stood in the queue as other travellers walked past her, bought tickets, and left. This was a matter of national pride. We offered to help her purchase a ticket. She was going to Manali, and now so were we. She had made the decision for us.

Off we left for Manali. Our bus conductor turned out to be an extremely helpful person. He told us that there were better places in Himachal Pradesh that we could go to. We decided to take his advice and we saw some of the most beautiful rural parts of the state. We got exposure to a very different culture because the areas had plenty of monasteries. We enjoyed ourselves so much that we ended up coming back after 15 days. Back in the office, everyone was so jealous of the lovely photographs we had brought with us.

I had a glimpse of heaven on that trip. The incredible beauty of the places blew me away. And it was a steal because we spent only INR 2,200 per person. I can't believe I remember so many details of that trip a few decades later. That's because it was an experience I will never forget. Everyone I travelled with is now busy in their own lives, including me, and all we have are memories. When I am asked about my favourite trip, this one to Himachal Pradesh comes to mind immediately. No vacation to Switzerland, Italy, Amsterdam, Austria, or any place in the US comes close to it.

## See You on My Side Soon

As I mentioned at the beginning, this is a book I wish I'd had when I was a young person on the cusp of adulthood. I wanted someone to share with me the path to faster success. Our 20s are when we set the foundation for our careers. A couple of misses at that age can cost us a few precious years. While some people can bounce back easily from those setbacks, it's not possible for everyone. That is why I wrote this book – so you can learn from my experience and reach your goals faster. I wish you success beyond your wildest expectations and I hope to see you as a professional soon. If this book has helped you, do let me know at therakeshsingh@gmail.com. I'd love to hear from you. Till then, all the best and break a leg.